RELEASE FROM POWERLESSNESS

A GUIDE FOR TAKING CHARGE OF YOUR LIFE

SECOND EDITION

Linda L. Moore, Ed.D.

Linda L. Moore & Associates

KENDALL/HUNT PUBLISHING COMPANY
4050 Westmark Drive   Dubuque, Iowa 52002

Cover image courtesy of Corel.

Copyright © 1991, 2004 by Linda L. Moore

ISBN 0-7575-0957-6

Printed in the United States of America

10 9 8 7 6 5 4 3 2 1

For
Alice Sargent
my friend, colleague, mentor

February 5, 1939–June 5, 1988

CONTENTS

Acknowledgments

I want to express deep gratitude to the many friends and colleagues who have helped and supported me as I have worked on this book. Years ago four people encouraged me to write—Earl Glosser, Jeannette Brown, Bill Eddy, and especially the late Alice Sargent, to whom this book is dedicated.

The following individuals I thank for reading the manuscript in its early stages and/or encouraging me along the way: Kay Barnes, Natasha Josefowitz, Harriet Lerner, Anne Wilson Schaef, Diane Fassel, Deborah Garnett, Merle Moores, Carolyn Desjardins, Annette Morgan, Elizabeth Brennan, and Paula Echohawk.

Gerald Whetstone, former Associate Editor for Kendall-Hunt made the publication of this book possible. He encouraged and supported me at every difficult stage of the process, willingly spending extra time when I felt stuck.

Finally, I thank my brother, Rick Moore, for constant support.

Dr. Linda L. Moore, President
llmoorepsy@worldnet.att.net

PROLOGUE

When *Release From Powerlessness* was published in 1991, I was filled with enthusiasm for women's potential—to take charge, to retrieve power in every arena of life. Today, at the beginning of the new millennium, while pleased by the astonishing successes of women everywhere, I am discouraged by the similarity in the problems women face—personally and professionally. The "same old dilemmas" existed 10 years ago, 20 years ago, even 30 years ago, when I first began to think and speak about women and power. Does my perception of the "same thing" cause me to wonder what's wrong? Yes! And the answer is not in more suggestions of how to "fix women." There is nothing wrong with us! There is, however, a great deal wrong with the systems in which we live and work. Some systems have changed; others are changing slowly. Far greater changes are needed if girls and women are to lead healthy lives filled with powerful options and life giving equity.

Anthropologist Helen Fisher, in *The First Sex*, tells us that the combination of demographics, the service oriented direction of our world, and the more global way women think (Fisher calls it Webbing) put women in perfect position to assume leadership in almost every area of work. That perspective excites me; however, the week I was reading it, I was conducting a workshop on the East Coast and heard a beleaguered 25 year old's example of giving power away. She slept with her boss. Not because he demanded it, and she was afraid she'd lose her job. That never entered her mind. She did it because she was worried if she said no, he'd think she didn't like him. The question is not "what's wrong with her?" The question is "what are we teaching young women at home and at school and in the media?" How are we preparing them to step into each new stage of life confidently, powerfully?

Unfortunately, we are teaching most of the same things we have taught for generations. Women are taught to give power away. Women are taught to focus most of their energy on building relationships and achieving identity through those relationships. Consequently, when such valued connections are threatened by conflict—minor differences or issues of great consequence—most women acquiesce, accommodate, please the other person, choosing a pseudo sense of intimacy, rather than risk disconnection by expression of self. I emphasize "pseudo" because the authenticity in any relationship suffers when the feelings, opinions, thoughts and desires of one dominate, and those of the other disappear.

What are women afraid of? Disapproval, criticism, anger, guilt, not being liked or loved are the most common answers I hear. Beyond these feelings that arise primarily from faulty thinking, there are hard realities in our culture that create genuine fears. Every nine seconds a woman in the United States is battered. Reproductive rights are under siege daily, and currently our government is withdrawing funds for United Nations family planning. Additionally our government is hesitating to sign international documents supporting equality for women all over the world. The gains of Title IX are being threatened. Even though many women have made significant and exciting strides in all areas of life, violence directed at women is at an all time high. We are the fastest growing poverty group in the world, the fastest growing group of homeless, the fastest growing group of illiterates. Something is wrong with the system. Women, as a group, are still regarded as powerless.

The potential for the transcendence of gender differences regarding powerlessness seems more possible in times of national crisis. We are at war, and we are faced with the possibility of continued war with other countries, as well as considerable damage to our alliances all over the world. It is in these times that we see the damage of violence, suffered primarily/dominantly by our young men, and thus are tempted to overlook the necessity to analyze what happens to women. The solution is to examine the ways in which our systems damage both women and men.

The messages of a "dominator culture" continue to be passed on, making it essential for each individual to learn to release themselves from powerlessness and to work with other women and men in the process of self and system healing.

The original version of *Release From Powerlessness: A Guide for Taking Charge of Your Life* outlines steps for beginning that process for women. As I speak about power all over the country, and reflect on the stories I'm told by women who've read the book, I find that the theories, ideas, and techniques are still urgently relevant. Consequently there are no major changes to the theory and content of the body of the book. There are additional ideas in the Epilogue, additions to reading lists and resources—and a plea to all of us to pay more attention to what is happening to all women everywhere.

The original reading recommendations are the same because they, too, are still relevant. Three books I most frequently suggest were written ten to twenty years ago: *The Assertive Woman* by Nancy Austin and Stanlee Phelps and *The Dance of Anger* and *The Dance of Intimacy* by Harriet Lerner. The additions in the resource section are books that have altered my perspective, challenged my thinking and caused me to ask "What else am I missing or failing to comprehend?"

A final section has been added to the book. There I emphasize some important things for us to focus on, think about, and act on. Read as much as you can, attend workshops, do things that stretch you and pull you outside the box the system has structured and defined for you. Power resides first in seeing and understanding. It is then expressed in action.

METAPHOR

Frequently, I think and speak in metaphors. Verbal pictures or visual images draw on our mind, emotions, and experiences, forming a connection that is like a bridge. The connecting bridge joins the right and left hemispheres of the brain deepening understanding. When that connection occurs, I usually experience (or hear others express) that all important "ah-ha." So, I have chosen one special picture to share with you. It is my personal image of release and movement toward positive expression of power. As you read this book, I hope you will find an image that works for you.

> I am sitting by a small, quiet pond. The pond is perfectly calm. The sun is setting and I am trying to come to rest, to relax. I try and when I do, ripples appear in the pond. Images pop up everywhere, almost as if they are rising from the water itself. The "shoulds" of my life drive and whirl around my brain in a rapid procession of circles.
>
> How can I feel better, I ask? I ponder. I struggle. Finally, the answer comes from someplace deep inside me. A voice I have not heard before speaks to me, "Get up and move." I rise up and begin to walk around the pond. Suddenly, as if compelled to do so, I am running. My body is sweating and glistening in the remaining light. The muscles stretch and break free from tension. I run harder, flinging my arms. I feel flushed, free, open, safe, and strong, and I feel *release.*
>
> The ripples quiet again and I see my reflection. I am myself. I am. Everything is.

INTRODUCTION

The feelings from which we seek relief are basic—pain, anger, fear, loneliness, and shame. Holding on to such feelings or "stuffing" them rather than experiencing or expressing them causes distorted thinking and dysfunctional behavior. We do things or say things that are not in our best interest or, perhaps, even harmful to us. The non-expression of feelings over time leads to a general state of powerlessness. We feel we are not the people making decisions about our lives. Powerlessness feels like, "I'm out of control"; "Everything is falling apart"; "I don't know who is in charge, but it's not me!"; "I feel helpless to change"; "I am STUCK!"

At one time or another in our lives, we find ourselves struggling with one, if not all of these feelings. To understand them as normal parts of our process is essential in moving toward health, joy, love, recovery, and internal authority. For women this can pose a dilemma because many of our deepest authentic feelings are labeled by society as abnormal, our more important experiences as insignificant. With such value judgments, it is hard, painful, and sometimes scary to freely talk about real feelings or experiences.

Often our lives have been devalued or negatively labeled because they are so different from the lives of men. We must begin to own our lives and our emotions for what they are, as they are, in order to value the positive. We must begin to "release" ourselves from what keeps us mired, what keeps us from moving to full potential. We can no longer evaluate ourselves using men as the yardstick.

Thankfully, during the last 30 years, women's stories have finally been told by researchers, authors of fiction, journalists, and psychologists. We have begun to understand that most women think and feel differently, and deal with the world differently than most men. We can now identify differences in both our moral development and in how we approach learning, knowing, and living. As you and I look around we are able to see our women friends, our peers, lovers, and work associates in wide-ranging, varied conditions of life. We can see the repression, the expression, the missed or developed potential, the defeats, the successes. We need this knowledge and understanding of the historical and current conditions of our lives if we are to know what it is we are moving toward.

Powerlessness is a key part of the cultural inheritance of women. The lives we lead are defined by a belief that women have no power. This is our external reality. Powerlessness is also our internal experience; we are socialized to give our power away. The interaction of the internal and external results, all too frequently, is a condition of paralysis for women. This state of paralysis keeps us from recognizing our feelings, from acting on our feelings, and primarily from taking care of our own inner needs.

This state of powerlessness is a condition we most often identify as we look outside ourselves. Externally, we know we are seeing powerlessness when a women is raped and almost killed in Central Park in New York City; when thousands of women are forced to flee violent households and to seek shelter for themselves and their children; when women in India are burned to death to allow their husbands to find wives with a larger dowry; and, when a fetus is aborted in China because it is female. It is much harder to see powerlessness inside ourselves.

Powerlessness keeps us in denial about all the other emotions that so deeply need to be expressed by women. Most women experience deep levels of pain and most have managed to mask or medicate their pain. The paradox here is the myth in this culture that women can easily express their emotions and that expression is accepted. The reality is that women are only marginally able to express what they are feeling and are rarely validated for their feelings. Some women feel comfortable crying in the movies, showing emotion when other people are in pain or hurt, and generally, just being more "emotive." The real pain experienced by women is far less freely expressed. In fact, very few individuals are willing to see, hear, and share the deep levels of pain experienced by the majority of women in this culture.

While the roots of such pain are debatable, I have come to believe in my work with hundreds of women in individual and group therapy, in workshops, in consulting relationships, and in audiences across the country, that this pain comes from a loss of the authentic self—the real you. The feelings, desires, ideas, preferences, and opinions that are genuinely yours become more quiet, remote, and gradually hidden. As you give up "the self," powerlessness surges. Giving up self means taking on someone else's definition of what you should feel, think, desire, believe or prefer. This is an aspect of codependence; an alienation from the authentic self and an other-directed or people-pleasing posture.

Section I of this book discusses a theory that a pattern of denial of the authentic or true self leads to powerlessness; that powerlessness necessitates the development of a pseudo or false self and over time creates and cements a state of codependence. Further, codependence, untreated and powerlessness, unacknowledged, leads to addictions. Consequently, the understanding of the links of powerlessness, codependence, and addictions becomes vital to our expression of a healthy, evolving self. In Chapter 1 women and our relationships with power are explored; Chapter 2 discusses the specific effects of powerlessness on our lives; Chapter 3 defines codependence and the relationship to powerlessness; and Chapter 4 discusses powerlessness and addictions.

Section II introduces techniques for self-analysis. Chapter 5 gives questions for getting started and provides a self-system analysis. Self-system refers to a balanced analysis of problems. A problem may be "self-based," as "I need to change," or a problem may be "system-based," as "I need to intervene or change my situation, environment, or system." Chapter 6 identifies therapeutic metaphors and questions to assist you in your inner journey. Chapter 7 defines positive uses of power and Chapter 8 summarizes holistic steps for releasing power. These steps incorporate the total self (physical, emotional, intellectual, and spiritual) and help to provide movement in the direction of being the healthy powerful person you are capable of being. The last chapter, Chapter 9, is about men. It highlights basic differences between women and men and identifies the confining and limiting aspects of the male role.

This book is designed to help you explore, to help you ask questions, and to help you find answers. You will be asked to think, reflect, and to move to health by identifying your powerlessness, your codependence, and possibly your addictions. The best way to read the book is from front to back.

At the beginning of each chapter you will find anonymous quotations from women throughout the country that reflect their attitudes toward power. In each chapter there are either exercises to complete, questions to answer, or ideas on which to reflect. All are intended to create new levels of awareness for you. Try them. Write and reflect on each chapter's information before you move to the next.

Additionally, this book is about providing guidelines and support for your journey. It reflects my personal journey and the journeys of my women clients and friends; our thoughts, questions, experiences and struggles. This book does not offer shortcuts, rather a road map for your journey. I want to hear about your personal journey and triumphs.

Section I

Understanding Powerlessness, Codependence, and Addictions

CHAPTER 1

WOMEN AND POWER

"I feel that I keep myself from being powerful by not having enough confidence in my ideas even though they may be good ones. Another way, is by having a fear of exhibiting my anger in a situation. I keep myself from being powerful by holding back my opinions when they are negative rather than expressing them to others. I feel I keep myself from being powerful when I let another manager (especially a male) handle a problem instead of taking care of it myself."

"I always compromise. I have a difficult time learning to 'love and fight.' Fear of being wrong."

"Behavior that was programmed in as a child. Don't let them know you're smarter than they are, don't overwhelm them."

One of the unfortunate side effects of growing up female is that you may be at least 30 years old, sometimes older, before you discover it is really okay to "color outside the lines."

For a moment, take yourself back to the first grade and remember how Miss Smith or Miss Jones validated and praised you for staying inside the lines when you colored. You may be able to recall taking a darker color crayon and outlining the picture before you colored inside. A client once explained she did that to hide any mistakes she might make. Most adults fear making mistakes, and the fear begins in childhood.

The disapproval of others affects learning and behavior. It is easier to guarantee the teacher's approval by being careful. The reward is for being neat and perfect. To be perfect takes time and caution. Contrast that perfection: the little boy sitting next to you wasn't coloring inside the lines. He was likely scribbling all over the paper!

What does this difference in behavior have to do with power? It's an example of how girls begin to learn the importance of control—staying inside the box that defines and contains the female role; respecting vs pushing at boundaries and limits defined by the box; living life the way others say you should; learning risk—taking is frightening and dangerous. Coloring outside the lines represents letting go and risking.

As a female, efforts to color outside the lines, to do something that is not in accord with the norms of growing up female, generally results in being punished. Consequently most women become overly compliant. A belief develops: if you are a very good girl, if you are nice to people, if you say the right things, if you work as hard as you possibly can, then everything will be okay. In other words, everything will turn out right because the world is fair. Cautiously clinging to such myths impedes the development of a sense of power.

Generally, boys and men learn to push at boundaries. They learn coloring outside the lines can be more enjoyable. They are rewarded for learning the broad brush strokes of life. They learn to take risks; to push against rules and authorities and to have a greater sense of who they are in the external world, in relation to the world of work, and power.

Power Defined

Power is best understood when broken into two categories: positional power and personal power.

Positional power is the power available to you based on your placement in the hierarchical structure and the label attached to your position. Picture any organization you work in, live in, or relate to and the levels or rungs of management. Mark your own location and identify your position in the structure of the hierarchy. You may be the president, the director, the chairperson of a task force, the executive secretary or you may be an employee. Your label and your position in the hierarchy indicates your ability to reward and to punish, to hire and to fire. Positional power can also be acquired from expertise. You may be in a position of power that is somewhat lower in the hierarchy, but when called in to a top-level meeting where you are the expert on the subject being discussed, your positional power increases. Additionally, positional power can be acquired as a result of having money. If you are wealthy, your money can give you access to the top people in almost any organization or corporation in your community or society.

Positional power is the category of power most women are told they should pursue. Many women are working hard to develop the expertise to move up the ladder, to acquire more positional power. Some women, on the other hand, question how much positional power they want. When organizations are not healthy, this is an essential question. Perhaps most importantly, some women are beginning to search inside themselves, and in discussions with other women, for new models for the use of positional power in our organizations.

The second category of power, personal power, is far more important for women. Personal power is the ability to create your own environment. Take the definition of personal power further by asking several questions. Who is in charge of your life? Who is in charge of the way your day goes? Who is in charge of the way your week is managed, or the way this month has felt to you? Who has been in charge of this year and its activities? Who is responsible for the direction your life is taking? When you ask who is in charge, you must also ask: Is it me? Is it my spouse or partner? Is it the significant other person I live with? Is it my boss? Is it my two-year old, my sixteen-year old, or my mother? Possibly it is a committee, of all those identified, that convenes weekly to decide what you should do!

For most women, most of the time, the answer to this question is: "Someone besides me is in charge of my life." If your answer is not that strong, it may instead be: "I am not in charge enough of the time." Again, because we have not learned or at least don't remember that we can color outside the lines, we let other people direct our lives. Often, we do not take responsibility for the fact that each of us does create our own life, even if through indecision.

Often, we have not been taught how to assume the responsibility for the direction our life takes. We are socialized to *give our power away*. We let others make choices and decisions for us. We don't do anything as ridiculous as saying, "Here, take all of my personal power and manage it; tell me what to do." We are socialized more subtly to let other people take the lead, to set the goals, to make the decisions. The process of giving power away is like yearly soil erosion. Each time we "hold on" to an important feeling or thought, or don't act, some of the richness of self is lost. But because each incident of giving in—giving power away—seems small or insignificant, the overall effect, the reality that the soil is becoming arid, isn't observed until it is almost life-threatening.

We become significantly other-directed as females, and in that process, we grow up without a full understanding of our inner selves, of who we are. As adults, we feel a void, an emptiness, and a sense of not really understanding where we are going. We may simply feel lost! Not being able to determine our own pathways, we become frightened and confused. We hold on more, and harder, to what is familiar and give away more power.

Relationships and Power

What are the behaviors specific to giving power away? To understand this, take a look first at the importance women place on relationships.

A significant part of our socialization process, as women, is learning to value relationships. We are taught to make them the center of our universe, our primary focus. Men, on the other hand, are socialized to see work or tasks and themselves as the center of the universe, their primary focus.

There is nothing wrong with having relationships as your central focus in life. It is an extremely positive part of female socialization. However, for most women, it is taken too far. An imbalance develops. Because we value relationships so deeply, we avoid conflict. We give up our personal power because we so deeply fear being in conflict with significant others in our lives. We may also fear being in conflict with "insignificant" others—for example, the man who is trying to sell encyclopedias or aluminum siding on the telephone!

If you are going to have personal power, you will almost always be in conflict to some degree. Conflict may be only a slight disagreement or mild argument or it may be a serious confrontation. It may be something as simple as saying what you feel, what you want, what you need, what your idea or your opinion is. For most women, such expression is an extremely difficult and sometimes even painful thing to do. Consequently, we find many ways of avoiding conflict, and in this process, we hold on or stuff real feelings and thoughts down deep inside. What we do is give away our personal power. We do not accept the responsibility for creating our own lives because we generally do not know how.

The effect of giving power away can be dramatic. For many women there is deep self-alienation; a sense of worthlessness; an intense resentment of the people you spend so much time taking care of; a feeling of not having any idea of where you are going and what you are doing; a condition of total fatigue; and, a general state of holding on tightly to keep everything from flying apart.

If these symptoms indicate the price women are paying, it is obvious we need to take back our personal power. Re-owning our personal power is essential for our physical, intellectual, emotional, and spiritual well-being, and for our professional and personal success.

If it is true that you give away personal power, then it is also true you can get it back. Part of your self-analysis has to do with understanding to whom you have given it, how that has happened, the effects on you, and finally, what you need to do.

The people in your life to whom you have given your personal power won't give it up easily. When you begin to take it back, you will experience fear. Conflicts will undoubtedly surface. Retrieving personal power is difficult and cannot be done all at once. It is not as simple as announcing: "I'm taking back all my personal power!"

If you have been "coloring inside the lines" most of your life, the first time you take a step to retrieve personal power will be a difficult one because you may be confused about how you want to define your "separateness," in a healthy way, from all the people around you. Begin gradually with an assessment of what is going on in your life, how it feels to be aware of this concept, and what it is you really want to do. Move slowly, a step at a time, a day at a time.

Historical Perspective

If we look historically at our role as women, it is clear many of us have pushed against the traditionally defined boundaries for being female. The boundaries have been determined by society and its institutions. Society then operates somewhat like a huge umbrella, covering us with social and cultural expectations and giving us both signals and specific information on how to behave.

Think about institutions broadly. Think of your family, the place you work, the church, schools, government, the PTA or any organization or institution with which you have regular contact.

With each of these institutions you have a prescribed role. For example, in the institution of the family, your role is "daughter." It might include "sister" and possibly "wife" and "mother." In an organization, your role may be employee or employer; chairperson of the board or department head. A role is a specific set of expectations for your behavior when you occupy a position in a social group. Being a daughter is a role in the social group we call family.

For every role prescribed for you by the institution there is a set of expectations. Rules and expectations from those roles are important because they prescribe what you must do to be an acceptable member of the group. Consider the traditional roles of wife and mother and the attached expectations. Behaviors immediately pop into your mind when you think about what a good wife or a good mother does. Right now, on a sheet of paper, list the roles you play and the rules and expectations for each.

As we learn to identify with the roles we play, we use the roles and role expectations as a way of determining whether or not we are measuring up. You can quickly identify failure to meet role expectations because of the phenomenon called psychological group pressure. When you behave outside your role expectations, you experience group pressure. The pressure comes from the definition of *appropriate* or *good* given by a specific group. For example, "good mothers" can be extremely disapproving of "bad mothers." "Good employees" can be highly critical of "bad employees."

Perhaps you have never married, never had children, live with another woman, or work in a non-traditional, male-dominated field. If so, the critical attitudes of people uncomfortable with "differences" are obvious.

The earliest messages of criticism, "You aren't doing it right," came from your family of origin—mother, dad, siblings, or primary caregivers adults who influenced you. Perhaps you experienced comments such as these: "You look very nice, dear, but don't you think your skirt is a little too short?" or "Aren't you going to wear some lipstick?" "Can't you find nicer friends?" "You'll never amount to anything if you don't _____." Or maybe when you acted on a difficult decision, you heard, "How can you do this to me?" "You are always thinking of yourself. You're selfish." Today, regardless of your age, disapproval may still come from your family of origin and from the internalized tapes of what a family member has said to you about your behavior, your life.

As an individual in our society you must interact with dozens of institutions/organizations. Your behavior is expected to "fit" the roles and expectations prescribed. Traditionally, women have looked to society for definitions of appropriate behavior. They have behaved as expected and been validated for compliance. In the past there has been very little observable tension or discord between women and their prescribed roles and behaviors.

However, in the last 30 years, women have begun individually and as members of groups to question the expectations of society. Women have questioned the traditional definitions of female roles. They have begun to challenge these roles as limiting, as sometimes uninteresting, and frequently as unfeeling. Consequently, women in general have found themselves in conflict with almost every institution in their culture.

Think for a moment about all the roles prescribed for you. Imagine each one is represented by a small, square box. Visualize yourself inside a box—it represents roles and expectations that define you and likely limit your uniqueness. Today many women feel trapped inside these boxes. Imagine what happens, perhaps what has happened to you, as you have attempted to move outside the boundaries of a box. See yourself stick a hand or a foot outside. As you attempt it, outside forces come from opposing directions, trying to force you back inside. For most women, this is a familiar process. We know when we do things differently, someone or some group will be there to criticize, to punish, and sometimes to threaten our lives. Self-esteem is threatened, individual perceptions are challenged, and sometimes jobs are lost and relationships destroyed.

In the lives of many women, escaping the confines of the box has become crucial for mental health and emotional well-being. How do you get out of the box? Build perspective—not by fleeing the box and losing the psychological framework and support for identity, but rather by going outside the box, climbing up on top and sitting there where you can see.

The boundaries of the boxes are needed as a psychological frame of reference for who you are. The question is who defines the boundaries? Who has defined your role? You? Society? Is your boss, husband, partner or significant other defining your role? Have you allowed your family of origin to hold onto that responsibility?

Perhaps the most important psychological and behavioral issue for us to understand is that institutions identify women *as a group* as powerless. Initially, this is a shocking concept, an untrue, even ridiculous statement. If you search for exceptions to this idea, you'll, thankfully, find a few examples of relatively new institutions, not our traditional ones. They are the networks created by women for women. They are organizations managed or owned by women (or have as their main function providing services to women). Or they are a growing number of organizations which have begun a process called "organization transformation." Other than these few exceptions, a continued analysis of the institutions in our culture will show that they define women as powerless.

Today *individual* women more frequently emerge as powerful in organizations/institutions. You can identify a handful of women who have community visibility or national visibility—women with power. There may be powerful women in your own family. Historically women who have had power at any time and in any institution have had it largely because of their personal power. Power institutionally prescribed and identified has not and does not exist for women, individually or as a group on any large sociocultural basis. Power exerted as a result of personal power and the ability to exercise it has always been with us.

Institutional Powerlessness

What does institutional powerlessness mean? First, it means you must lead your life interacting with institutions and with people who believe you have no power. Consequently you are in a constant struggle to gain power, even if it is an unconscious struggle. It means you must fight for the recognition you receive. It means you must struggle with authority figures and institutions that always question: (1) whether you know what you are talking about; (2) whether you have the authority to say what you are saying; and (3) how a woman got into the position that you are in.

Institutional powerlessness means you are under continual stress and strain. Each woman, in her own way, learns to adapt to heightened stress. Most of us have become so accustomed to the results of powerlessness, to the stress we must deal with as a result of that definition, that we no longer recognize the amount of energy it takes to handle the behavior or the conditions that powerlessness produces. Imagine for a moment the amount of energy you have diverted from other sources in order to handle the stress that comes from the kind of life you have as a powerless person. Imagine further what you might have been able to accomplish by now if you had been able to use that energy for yourself.

As women living in the new millennium, we find ourselves functioning in institutions that do not recognize the changing roles of women. There is still no large-scale institutional recognition or approval for who we are and the choices we have made for our lives today.

What is institutional recognition? Institutional recognition can best be defined by a few examples.

(1) When you interview for a job one of the first things your prospective employer will mention is the wonderful day-care center available on-site. S/he will further describe numerous and excellent options for day-care throughout the community. A weekly allotment of at least ($200) per child per week is described as a job benefit. (The same information is given to men.)

(2) Maternity leave is described to you.

(3) Paternity leave is described to you.

(4) The freedom to leave work when you have a sick child or sick elderly family member (or the ability of your spouse, partner, or significant other to do the same) is described to you.

(5) Job-sharing options are described as a legitimate choice.

(6) Time-flex opportunities are outlined.

(7) Longer vacations, at least six weeks a year, are identified.

(8) On-site opportunities for relaxation, exercise, and healthy eating are identified and described.

(9) In general, "workaholic" expectations are non-existent.

These are just a few examples of what it would be like if our institutions respected the changes taking place for years in the lives of women. Our day-to-day lifestyles would be more manageable and we would be relieved of some stress from responsibility and tasks we now take on all by ourselves.

Most women live and work in institutions that pretend that it is still 1950. The institutional image is that by 10 o'clock in the morning, you've gotten the kids off to school, are enjoying your second cup of coffee, and preparing to tune into your favorite talk show. Your biggest concern is your reflection in your "Joy—washed" dishes!

Following World War II and through the 50's, the largest percentage of families in our culture were those which lived a traditional lifestyle: the husband worked outside the home, the mother worked inside the home and parented two to five children. These prescribed roles were validated by the culture. The new roles which have emerged are more likely to have developed through the experimental, risk-taking behavior of individuals and small groups of women. They are seldom validated by the culture or by institutions.

Women are leading different lives. The gap between *what is* and *what was* creates a tension that leaves some women feeling a little "crazy."

Large scale change crates a great gap—institutions are slow to catch up to individual change. What has happened to us as a result of this great lag? The primary result for women in the 80's was the image of a "Superwoman."* Once she emerged—alive and well, her cape flowing in the breeze, she has remained. Today we call it "achieving balance." When there is a condition where institutions are static and roles change rapidly, the gap must be filled. In the case of the changing roles of women, the gap has been filled by the women themselves, thus creating the expectation, the demand, for each of us to be a superwoman.

You cannot be superwoman without making yourself ill. Just as women in the past have given away power by not asserting their identity in work, personal life, and relationships, today women are giving away power when taking on numerous additional roles.

Relationship of Personal Power to Positional Power

For women interested in more positional power, in being leaders in organizations in our culture, your answer is first in personal

---

*For detailed information see *The Superwoman Syndrome* by Marjorie Shaevitz.

power. Many women achieve positional power before adequately developing their personal power. This is a setup for failure, or for tremendous amounts of unnecessary stress. It is difficult to succeed in a position of power without being aware of your personal power quotient.

If personal power and positional power are so heavily intertwined, what is the effect on behavior if positional power is achieved without developing personal power? If personal power has not been developed, you are uncomfortable or ill-at-ease in positions of power. You have difficulty in making things happen, in telling people what to do, in directing and delegating, in decision-making, in moving forward, in taking action, in taking risks. These behaviors or activities demand experience and skill development, but more importantly, an inner sense of self. Consider this example:

> Anne, highly talented and skilled, but with underdeveloped personal power gradually moves up the organization ladder. Anne has always been mildly uncomfortable in a position of authority, not really trusting her inner sense of self or her skills, so increased responsibility and power add stress and eventually more self doubt. Her discomfort may never show, except to the perceptive colleague. She begins to take on more responsibility, delegates less, isolates, works longer hours, resents other successful women in the organization, is often tense and irritable, develops numerous physical stress symptoms, has less time for her personal life, dislikes work she once loved, and feels confused. She may ask herself, "Is this where I was going?" "What do I really want?"

An inner sense of self and the expression of the self equals personal power. Unfortunately the process for socializing women does not encourage a strong knowledge of self and does not teach the skills for personal or positional power. Growing up in a culture that defines you as powerless deprives you of learning positive uses of power. You are, instead, more likely to learn negative uses of power. You learn "survival tools" which are generally passed on from mothers to daughters.

Negative Uses of Power

Early in life, women are taught at least three negative uses of power for manipulating men: (1) mothering them, (2) seducing them, and (3) acting childlike and helpless.

Take for example, an individual woman who acts childlike and helpless to get someone to do something for her rather than asking directly for what she wants. The legitimate request, a desire or need for assistance, is hidden. The indirect behavior discounts both the self and the reality of a legitimate need. Think of a time in your recent past when you have wanted help. A man has walked into the room and rather than asking directly for assistance, you suddenly find that you are behaving as if you are 10 years old, incompetent at the task before you. Such behavior evokes protective or nurturing behavior in many men and they will immediately move in to assist you with the task. Asking for and receiving help is okay. However, manipulating by being indirect about what you need is a negative use of power.

The seduction process is also familiar to most women. Again, rather than asking directly for what is needed, the woman behaves in a sexual manner to entice the man to assist her. This can include "innocent" batting of eyes, touching a man, flirting with him, and in unfortunate instances, being willing to sleep with a man in exchange for something really important.

Mothering men is also familiar to most of us. This usually involves "overdoing it"—or doing things for men they could do for themselves. Good examples include bringing them coffee, straightening their desks, interpreting how they are feeling, checking on them to see if they are okay. Then, when the woman feels the man is somewhat vulnerable, she may ask him for what she really wants, knowing he will feel obligated.

It is important to understand that the modes of behavior described here can also be healthy behaviors. It is healthy to be nurturing, to be sensual and sexual, and to be playful and childlike. Healthy behavior does not involve manipulation. Healthy behavior involves asking directly for what you desire.

Manipulative behaviors are survival tools learned early in life. They produce only negative power. Most women recognize these behaviors in themselves from time to time. Adults fall back on these behaviors in times of crisis when they do not know what else to do because they have not learned positive uses of power. These same tools or techniques carried into the office or into our casual or intimate relationships can be destructive. Women who recognize these behaviors usually mistrust each other when power is an issue. Men who have been manipulated by women fear falling prey again.

Negative Attitudes Toward Power

What other negative teachings are incorporated in our growing up? First, we may believe the myth that if I am power-*full,* you are power-*less.* In this myth, all the power in a particular interaction or relationship is thought to reside with one individual. If one person owns and exercises her own power then there may be little power available for whoever else may be involved. In reality, each of us can have as much power as we need, and as much as we are willing to risk obtaining for our use.

Second, we may learn that because we are female, there are "scarce resources." Being female means less is available to women in this culture than to most white males. There are fewer job opportunities, less time, less attention; there is less of almost everything available because women are not in the positions of power that allocate and assign such resources. While this would suggest that women compete with men for scarce resources there is a paradox. In fact, we compete with one another, other women, for these limited resources. We learn from a very early age to compete with one another for men and their attention and for limited educational and job opportunities. We see each other as our major source of competition.

Learning to be competitive with one another affects our psychological development. Many women report a great deal of confusion about their feelings when they see other women becoming successful. Feelings of being depleted or less worthwhile may surface resulting in a feeling of being less of a person. Such negative feelings "eat away" at self-esteem, but are a logical outcome of competing with other women for scarce resources. Historically, our legal system has structured this competition into the lives of women. Not so long ago when women applied for admission to college there was a quota on the number of women admitted. Thus, women competed with one another. Such behavior is against the law now, but we can still find subtle forms of discrimination.

If the negative feelings described sound familiar, acknowledge the feelings. If you occasionally wish that other women were not accomplishing more than you, let yourself be in touch with those feelings. Understand that your reaction is from your socialization, and then begin to work toward eliminating, healing, and dealing with such feelings. When other women accomplish great things in our culture, it can do nothing but enhance and empower the potential of all women.

A third teaching that we grow up with is a negative attitude about power and the behaviors associated with being powerful. We believe that men don't like women who are powerful, that other women don't like women who are powerful, and that being powerful or being competitive is not feminine. The reality is that, indeed, many men and women reject women who exercise their personal and positional power, but they are not behaving from a healthy center. Thus, when you exercise your personal power in a healthy, straight-forward way, you may experience conflict. With practice, you can gradually learn to handle the conflicts, judgments and/or rejections in a centered, healthy manner. As you grow to respect yourself, you will find that others will respect you, too.

Exercising personal power in a healthy, straight-forward way is difficult without understanding the society and its definitions of and beliefs about women. Seeing the reality of a history of powerlessness for women as a group is often difficult. However, it is the first step in your path to healing. The second is understanding the individual and group outcome of this powerlessness.

Exploring, Questioning, Reflecting

1. As you begin a process of self-exploration, try this "self-anchoring exercise." It is designed to give you some general perspective on where you've been, where you are today, and where you would like to go.

   Think about where you were and what your life was like 10 years ago.

   a. Where were you living?
   b. What was going on in your personal life? What were your relationships like? Were you married, separated, divorced, living with someone? Did you have any kids? What were the relationships with your parents like?
   c. What was going on in your work life? What kind of job or career were you in? Did you do volunteer work? Were you in school? How did you feel about what you were doing?
   d. What were your goals and priorities?
   e. Were there any "burning issues" in your life? Was something so important to you that you would have marched in a demonstration? Would you have joined a special committee or campaign?
   f. What was your physical condition? Were you healthy? Were you pregnant? Were you experiencing illness or operations?
   g. What was your spiritual life like? Did you feel a connection with a higher power? Did you choose to call this higher power God?
   h. Did you feel you were a powerful person or a powerless person? Did you think about power at all?

   Now review and compare your answers from 10 years ago to today. How much change are you aware of in your life? Is the change positive? Is the change negative? How do you feel as you review what you've written?

Finally, project yourself 10 years into the future. Write what you would like to be able to say to yourself 10 years from now. What are your goals? What do you want to do, to be, to accomplish? Save everything you've written and refer back to it as you continue to read.

2. Think about taking risks—"coloring outside the lines." Did you take risks as a child? Do you take risks now? Do you define your own boundaries? How does it feel to think about taking the risk to ask for and get what you want? How would it feel to do it?

3. Reflect on how your day, your week, your year, your life is going. Identify the individuals who make the decisions or choices that affect what is happening to you. Make a list of these people. Write about your feelings. Keep the list so you can refer back to it when you are ready to think about making changes that support taking your power back.

4. List all of the organizations or institutions with which you have regular contact. Identify your role in each. Write down the expectations of the roles. Reflect on any conflicts you see between or among the roles or conflicts you feel inside yourself.

CHAPTER 2

THE EFFECT OF POWERLESSNESS

"Scared. Mental block in confrontational situation."

"Do not want to excell or exceed accomplishments of brothers, husband or son. They won't love me. I'm inferior. I will not affirm my right to fulfill myself."

"Playing the little, defenseless girl. I'm nobody. Helplessness. Always asking for reassurance."

Living in a society that defines women as powerless takes a serious and sometimes deadly toll on the individual female. There is a sense of adaptation, adjustment, accommodation, acclimation, and finally a holding back of the authentic self. As you strive to control yourself by holding on to strong feelings and thoughts, the genuine expression of self is stifled. The authentic self learns to hide somewhere inside.

Each of us knows and experiences the sense of holding on, holding back, or exerting physical and emotional energy to control. There are countless thoughts, ideas, feelings, and behaviors you decide not to express. Rather, you simply hold on to them, either because your judgment or intuition says it is a good idea or, you're afraid not to, or you have learned, over the years, to automatically hold on, to the point that you do not realize you do it.

Since all of us experience "holding on" to something sometime, it is important to explore how detrimental this process is or can become. How does "holding on" really affect your day-to-day life? How does "holding on" make you feel? How do you detect that you are holding on? The most basic symptom is "partial paralysis of the lower jaw." It happens like this: You are in a tense interaction with someone important to you. The conversation escalates. Your feelings, beliefs or preferences are strong, important to you. You grow frustrated as you realize the other person is not hearing you, not really listening. At the moment of confrontation, a crucial statement is required, and your entire lower jaw freezes—nothing comes out of your mouth. "What is happening to me?" might be your first thought, or "What's wrong with me"?

Your mind has frozen. Somewhere in the course of the conversation, probably out of your awareness, you began to experience fear—fear of losing, of not being heard, of almost anything. Fear stimulates old patterns of responding, and because many of us learned very early to "hold on," that is what your system begins to do. You prepare to protect yourself when you are scared. The fight/flight syndrome is triggered and blood rushes from your brain into your extremities, allowing you to fight or to flee. Your problem-solving and conversational skills are momentarily diminished. A primary response is to simply "hold on." Since this is a scenario experienced by most women at least once in a while, the question is how often does it happen? Is it infrequent or is it the story of your life? Are you in fact, defined by your inability to say what you want to say or do what you want to do?

The Results of Unexpressed Feelings

Visualize with me a metaphor of the "trash compactor." Your trash compactor contains all of your unexpressed feelings of anger, pain, fear, loneliness and shame, as well as unexpressed feelings of joy, love, enthusiasm and self-worth. It also holds your unexpressed thoughts, ideas, preferences, and opinions. The trash compactor fills the trunk of your body creating physical sensations throughout, in the stomach, solar plexus (upper middle part of the abdomen), chest, and throat.

Most women began holding on and storing their true feelings at a very early age. Those "looks" and verbal or physical expressions of disapproval taught most little girls to be afraid or at least uncomfortable with saying "this is what I feel, think, prefer, desire, believe, or hope."

Female socialization teaches you to be understanding, to be receptive to the needs and feelings of others, and to put those needs of others first. Coming "after" someone else is an acceptable and familiar way for women to function. Learned ways of behaving create hundreds of incidents in which we sit on feelings, beliefs, and needs in order to understand someone else or help someone else feel okay, or because we're afraid to say what we really want to say. Where do these unexpressed feelings go since they can't simply evaporate or disappear? They are stored in the internal trash compactor.

Over the years incident after incident piles up. Eventually women begin to experience this overloaded compactor through emotional rushes of anxiety or tension in situations of conflict. A feeling that something of intensity is weighing you down or rising in your body and threatening to emerge. In order to control the uncomfortable feelings (or compact the trash) you may hold your breath, swallow hard, count, or otherwise attempt to push your mind into a rational thought process. Thus, you begin to feel in control again.

As unexpressed feelings become larger in number and stronger in intensity, the compacting process becomes more difficult, no matter how hard you try. To cope with these difficulties some women choose to use a medicating substance such as alcohol, drugs or food to quiet the persistent rumble of unacceptable feelings. As an alternative to a substance, some women find relief through excessive TV viewing, spending too much money, working long hours, or escaping into a bad relationship. Whether a substance or a process is chosen, a progressive need to feel in control of the feelings will develop. As a result, the trash compactor continues to fill up, unexpressed feelings continue to be stored. Finally there is emotionally no more room to stuff feelings. Some or one of the following things may occur:

(1) An angry, emotional outburst, far out of proportion to the event, but one that reinforces the image of the irrational female who cannot control her feelings either at home or at work.

(2) A tendency to burst into tears at any time but especially when someone says something caring.

(3) Ongoing irritability—everything is annoying. Others may describe the behavior as "bitchy."

(4) Physical symptoms of some severity; such as, ulcers, gastritis, or colitis.

(5) Frequent physical illness—colds or flu that require bed rest and medication.

Any of these five responses allow the average woman to temporarily become distracted from some of the discomfort from unexpressed feelings. An angry outburst, a good cry, or a few days in bed will often clean out about one third of the trash compactor contents.

With the resulting relief, there can be a return to routine behavior until the unexpressed feelings build up and the trash compactor begins to feel full once again. This process results in a vicious cycle which allows no legitimate outlet for negative feelings. It is a system that encourages a woman to see herself as a victim and provides no apparent intervention for her to view herself otherwise. Additionally, as the cycle continues, feelings of craziness may develop. This craziness is typified by a lack of trust of perceptions, experiences, and feelings. Generally a woman questions what is really wrong with her basic nature. Self doubt leads to even more holding on, controlling, or holding back of unexpressed emotions.

This on-going cycle can lead to serious emotional and physical problems. Reaching your capacity for stuffing feelings (a full trash compactor) does not mean you are sick or crazy, but it is a serious warning from the total system that it is operating on overload, that something needs to be done.

A full or overloaded system affects you physically, emotionally, behaviorally, and spiritually, as indicated in the following lists. Experiencing multiple symptoms is an indication that professional consultation from a physician or psychologist may be needed to successfully intervene.

PHYSICAL SYMPTOMS ASSOCIATED WITH STRESS

Muscle tension, aches, spasms
Headaches or migraines
Skin rashes
Excessive tiredness/exhaustion
Insomnia
Shortness of breath or difficulty breathing
Dizziness or blurred vision
Ringing or buzzing in ears
Ulcers
Gastritis
Colitis
Chest pain or palpitations
Hypertension
Cancer—especially breast cancer
Change in blood and hormones

Other: List any physical symptoms you experience that are not listed here.

_____

_____

_____

_____

_____

_____

_____

_____

_____

_____

_____

EMOTIONAL/PSYCHOLOGICAL SYMPTOMS ASSOCIATED WITH STRESS

Worry/apprehension
Worry about being worried
General emotional tension
Agitation
Anxiety
Sadness
Depression
Excessive self-criticism/frequent discounting of self
Irritability
Anger
Rage
Helplessness
Hopelessness
Low self-esteem or self-worth

Other: List any emotional/psychological symptoms you experience that are not listed here.

_____

_____

_____

_____

_____

_____

_____

_____

_____

_____

_____

BEHAVIORAL SYMPTOMS ASSOCIATED WITH STRESS

Indecision
Difficulty acting on decisions
Preoccupation
Poor concentration
Poor time management
Frantic pace
Productivity loss
Superficial involvement—giving up
Absenteeism
Frequent unavailability
Difficulty in getting along with others
Excessive criticism of others
Change in eating and drinking habits
General negativity

Other: List any emotional/psychological symptoms you experience that are not listed here.

_____

_____

_____

_____

_____

_____

_____

_____

_____

_____

_____

SPIRITUAL SYMPTOMS ASSOCIATED WITH STRESS

Void
Emptiness
Dark hole inside
Panic
Feeling ungrounded
Overwhelming emotions
Rootlessness
Disconnected
Compulsions
Addictions

Other: List any spiritual symptoms you experience that are not listed here.

_____

_____

_____

_____

_____

_____

_____

_____

_____

_____

_____

_____

_____

_____

Negating the Self

Ironically the act of giving to others, something women are taught to do and to value, often becomes life-draining, keeping the authentic nurturing self from developing. The paradox is dramatic. It is important to distinguish the "ways" in which women are taught to give from the "act" of giving or nurturing.

Negating the self in a lifelong process of giving to others is giving away personal power. It is losing the authentic self. Negating the authentic self is holding back and consequently never discovering who you really are. Consider the emotional difference between giving because you should, you have to, you are supposed to, versus giving because you choose to. How do you tell the difference? In the early stages of learning the difference, use the following measurement: if following the act of giving to another person you feel like hitting the individual over the head with a baseball bat that is the "should or have to" kind. That is giving away your personal power. If after giving to another, it feels good, clear, and you still like the person, it was probably a healthy choice. As a beginning, that is all you really need to know. As you gain more practice in making choices that are good for you, the more subtle and specific processes will become clear.

Nurturing and loving from a position of powerlessness does not work. Each individual must have a deep and true sense of self through the owning of personal power in order to truly love and give to another individual. Love and compassion with no roots in healthy personal power simply cannot grow. The emptiness and loneliness often experienced in our most important and intimate relationships can sometimes be connected to this concept. When the authentic self is not expressed and developed in the relationship, the intimacy lacks an "essence"—it is as if you are not really present. The feeling is a lack, an absence, a hole inside that needs filling. A woman must love herself in order to fully love someone else.

A Different View of the Body

Frequently the emotions and physical symptoms of women are clearly connected. Often you can locate the sensations of uncomfortable and unexpressed feelings in specific parts of your body—the solar plexus, upper and lower abdomen, chest and heart area, and the throat. These areas represent the physical seat of conflict between power and compassion—the struggle to love from a position of powerlessness.

To understand this idea from a physical energy perspective, consider the Eastern concept of the Chakra* system. There are seven energy centers in the body called Chakras (pronounced Cha'-kra). The first, the root chakra, is located at the base of the spine and represents a sense of groundedness, of being in touch with your environment, of being able to negotiate in the world and take care of yourself. The second is the genitals. It represents your healthy sexual and sensual energy and your ability to express it. The third is located in the solar plexus. It is referred to as the power center or sometimes as the ego or the center of emotions. The fourth chakra is located in your chest. It is your heart, your compassion, your loving and nurturing energy. The truth center, the fifth chakra, is located in your throat. It represents the need to speak the truth (no wonder we swallow hard and often choke on our words!). The sixth chakra is labeled the third eye. It is located on your forehead and represents the ability to see clearly, to see the truth. The last, the seventh, is the crown chakra. It is located on the top of the head and symbolizes a connection with the universe, a higher power, all that is.

Eastern philosophy, psychology, and medicine believe these seven chakras, (these spinning wheels of energy) when open and flowing, represent the healthy system. When an energy center is "blocked" there is physical disease or discomfort and/or unexpressed, unprocessed emotions.

Note in particular the solar plexus, the third chakra, the center of power or ego, and the fourth chakra, the center of the heart, love and compassion. As women struggle with the conflicts

*For more information, see Diagram in Appendix B, *Agartha—A Journey to the Stars* by Meredith Lady Young, and *The Chakras* and *Esoteric Healing* by Zachary F. Lansdowne.

between owning personal power and being loving and nurturing in valued relationships, many get stuck right in the middle, not knowing what is best, where to turn, what to do. That spot around the heart and solar plexus in the body feels empty, like a black hole, and physical symptoms such as ulcers and gastritis, chest pains, heart palpitations, difficulty in breathing, and sometimes breast cancer are reported.

In general, our body is programmed to give an early warning when something is not functioning properly. This is an alien concept to most of us because we have been taught to ignore physical discomfort unless it is extremely painful or to medicate it quickly so we can proceed with whatever we are doing. A product advertisement chants, "Take _____ when you haven't got time for the pain." As we fail to notice and respond to the signals given by the body, those same signals intensify. The body is a bit like a cranky child unable to get needed attention. The more the child is ignored, the louder or more demanding the child becomes, and sometimes s/he will cause serious trouble to get attention. In other words, serious physical or emotional symptoms suggest that we have not been paying attention to the body's signals, to our unique needs for a long time. Unfortunately, the socialization process for women, the years of training to put others' needs first is a built-in process for ignoring the self. This guarantees that physical, emotional, behavioral, and spiritual stress will occur.

Perhaps the biggest surprise is how remarkably well women "appear" to function. Many women can continue to cope for long periods of time before stress symptoms pose serious problems. Those who are accustomed to pushing their mind, body, and spirit to hold up under the pressure of relentless amounts of stress are shocked and frightened when excessive overload can no longer be ignored. At this point ignoring the signals of the body is a part of the denial that masks the overload. In our society, to face the signals means: "I can't cope, I don't measure up, What is wrong with me? and/or, I can't let anyone see me like this." Consequently, you "cover up," putting energy into appearing as if you are functioning well. Sometimes the main person you fool is yourself.

The losses to self are great. There are losses to your relationships, families, volunteer and work settings, and to the culture as well. Think of where you would be in your life at this moment, how you would feel, if you had not had to divert so much energy into struggling with a society that defines you as a powerless individual. How would you feel if you had not been forced to use so much energy to cope with the stress surrounding your lifestyle. Stresses are inherent in adjusting, accommodating, acclimating, and changing to meet the external demands from people and institutions.

Healing from the stress that results from powerlessness is essential. Healing begins with increased awareness of self and the environment.

Exploring, Questioning, and Reflecting

1. The following is a basic awareness activity. Read through it and then try it.

   Sit in a comfortable and relaxed position. Place your hands on your legs or in your lap. Put your feet flat on the floor . Close your eyes. Now begin to breathe a little more deeply and slowly. Become aware of your breath. Imagine that you can see the air coming into your body through the bottom of your feet, flowing through your body, and releasing through the top of your head. As you breathe, let your attention move over your body from your head to your toes, noticing how each part feels to you. Are your shoulders loose or tense? The tension and rigidity you may notice is an example of holding on physically. Now see what it feels like to "let go." Breathe air into the tense part of your body, and imagine letting go of the tension, pain or discomfort as you release your breath.

   Now let your attention move to your thoughts, ideas or any visual image. Just be aware of the activity, the wide range of things that flash or the fixing on one thought or image. Some of these flashes will be of things that are troubling you, things you are concerned about or things you are holding onto for some reason. There may be a few thoughts or images that you have been blocking, not letting come to the surface. Eventually you may want to explore these thoughts. For now, just be aware. See yourself letting go of your thought, if only temporarily, and feel the quiet of letting go even if it lasts only for a minute or a second.

Next, do the same with your feelings. Let your attention move down inside, away from your head, and focus on what you are feeling—happy, joyful, sad, angry, lonely. Again, feelings you have been blocking may surface, or feelings that have not been fully expressed may flare up. You might even feel tearful. Just breathe, relax, and let yourself be aware.

Finally, let yourself make contact with your spiritual awareness. You may call this aspect of self your inner knowing, the wise person inside you, your higher power, or God. Be aware. Listen for that still voice inside you. Know this level of contact may take time to develop.

Complete this activity by taking a couple of deep breaths, and slowly, at your own pace, open your eyes and return to your awareness of the room. The goal is to be conscious of some of the ways you may be holding on (physically, mentally, emotionally and spiritually). Through this awareness you can gain an inner knowing of the state of holding on, and experience letting go, releasing. This activity is brief, and an easy starting point.

When you have completed this activity, take whatever amount of time you need and write down anything important. This is an exercise in "consciousness." The more regularly you practice it the more you will be able to identify when you hold on, and then how to let go.

2. Start a journal. Commit to write just one sentence daily on your awareness of your physical, mental, emotional and spiritual experiences.

3. Review the checklist of stress symptoms on pages 25–28. If you have identified numerous physical symptoms or one that feels more persistent or serious, it is advisable to call a physician. If your list of emotional, behavioral, and spiritual symptoms is long, consider making an appointment with a psychologist or social worker; talk with a minister; or share what's going on with a family member or good friend. Sharing with someone else provides some release and is an opportunity to get feedback.

4. If you desire a more detailed personal assessment, fill out the stress questionnaires in Appendix D.

CHAPTER 3

POWERLESSNESS AND CODEPENDENCE

"I can't help thinking that it's more important to be liked or to get along than to exercise power."

"Trying to do more than I really am able to cope with. Want to please and can't accept but feel deflated when criticized. Feel insecure. Get tired and want to take care of too many details—procrastinate."

"I'm living with a (husband) man that detests any form of power in his wife; so I always have the concern of 'how can I make a decision without showing any outward strength or power'—I try to suppress the feelings."

Codependence is powerlessness when it is pervasive enough to damage our emotional, intellectual, physical and spiritual well-being. It is an emotional state, a learned way of determining behavior based on pleasing others or directing attention to what others want from us. It is an alienation from the authentic self. Codependence is a way of relating. It is a mode of functioning in painful families. It is a phenomena impacting our organizations at all levels. Codependence is a cultural set of rules for behavior that we have learned to call normal. Within the context of powerlessness, codependence is giving up the "self" for another person, a substance or a process, or an organization or institution. It is giving away your personal power.

The concept of codependence emerged from work with addictions. It is viewed by many professionals as a disease process that can kill just as surely as, and frequently more rapidly, than alcohol or drug abuse or other substance or process addictions. To fully understand the concept of codependence and its significance, tracing the manner in which it develops is essential.

The Development of Codependence

When you first enter this life, you come equipped with a core self, an authentic self. Each of you has the ability and the need to experience and express joy, love, self-worth, anger, fear, pain, and loneliness. For most of you, these needs to experience and express feelings, either positive or negative, are inhibited by our culture and our style and philosophy of parenting and educating.

Early in the course of learning, growing and developing, the child feels a feeling, begins to direct it outward, and then experiences some form of disapproval, a negative response from an adult, usually a parent or family member. The disapproval is experienced physically and emotionally—a negative or disapproving expression, a punishing voice or critical statement, or a physical restraint or blow. Whatever the response, when negative, the little child clearly receives the message that to feel and express the authentic self is not acceptable. The decision is made to retract the authentic feeling, to push it back down inside, and instead, to project a feeling that receives acceptance and praise. Children are not stupid. They quickly learn what behavior will generate positive responses from adults. Little girls are particularly attuned to the verbal and non-verbal cues in relationships. Here the groundwork is laid for the development of the pseudo-self.

*considering a reference to additional inclusion of charts in Appendix B

The pseudo-self does not express authentic pain, anger, fear or loneliness but rather is thoughtful, obedient, kind, smiles, gives, cares, and nurtures, regardless of real feelings. The pseudo-self is the codependent self, the one who learns how to behave in acceptable ways, in ways that often negate the true self. The validation from the adults you love and depend on while growing up is much more important than how you feel. In fact, it is usually too frightening to continue to feel or behave in ways that contradict the expectations of the family, and compliance feels safer. There are obvious exceptions to this concept. For instance, many children act out rather than comply. However, even in the acting out, the authentic self is lost once again. The behavior is still directed toward impacting the adults, and the real feelings are masked and pushed down inside. Regardless of the direction of the behavior, compliance or rebellion, the external behavior does not match the true emotions inside the individual and s/he loses touch with them.*

It is hard to keep the authentic self locked up, to keep genuine feelings at bay, but you do it. You divert energy, deny, and find countless ways to push the authentic self further away. (In a later chapter this process and its relationship to the development of addictions will be explored.) However, as the individual continues the practice of denying the interior and real self and continues to receive validation for the false self, this exterior gradually becomes who you are.

Codependence does not develop from the normal parent-child conflicts or normal, every-day mistakes. It comes from repeated patterns and ongoing dysfunctional dynamics in the family. The process of developing codependent behavior does not occur only as a result of dramatic and traumatic experiences. It is just as likely to be a result of our day-to-day family interactions when they are dysfunctional.

Consider this scenario between parent and child: The child has had an accident on a bike. This is her first two wheeler so she is scared. Her knees are scraped and bleeding. She is in pain. Her bike is broken. As a result, she comes to the parent, crying

---

*See the Diagram of Development of Codependence (developed 1988) in Appendix B.

and scared. When the response of the parent is an attempt to get the child to stop crying, the parent may say, "That doesn't hurt." What the child hears is that her perception of pain is inaccurate. She also hears that mother/father sees the situation differently from the way she does. As she watches her parent, she may see facial expressions and body language that express disapproval. In this case, the parent may now say, "I told you not to ride your bike on that gravel road. If you had done what I told you, this wouldn't have happened." The child has been discounted. The child hears that her pain and her broken bike are her fault because she disobeyed. It is likely that she will now experience shame. She believes that she is at fault; somehow she is defective.

This situation may be complicated further when the parent responds to the continued crying with, "You wouldn't want _____, your friend, to see you like this, would you?" The intensity of the shame sharpens. The young girl believes that she has made her mother/father unhappy; and her feelings are unacceptable for other people to see. Under these conditions, the true feelings of the child don't have much of a chance. She is hurt and scared because of her physical pain and broken bike, but now the conflict she feels with her parent becomes more important. She begins to shape her behavior in a way to get a positive response from the parent. She stops crying, smiles, tells her mother/father that she is sorry, and as she complies with the needs of the parent, she quickly sees the result. The body language and facial expressions of the parent will probably change. The parents relax, voice tone softens, and finally, the child may get a hug. However, in this case, the hug comes not for the child's pain and fear but for her compliance—her shaping up.

These kinds of dysfunctional interactions between the child and the parent repeated over and over in all aspects of life, contribute to the development of codependence. For this reason, the family dynamics in dysfunctional and/or alcoholic families must be examined to further understand the development of codependence.

Psychologist Robert Subby and John Friel in *Co-Dependency and Family Rules* (1984) have identified eight rules that are believed to teach, support, and maintain codependency:

(1) It's not okay to talk about problems.
(2) Feelings should not be expressed openly.
(3) Communication is best if indirect with one person acting as messenger between two others (triangulation).
(4) There are unrealistic expectations—be strong, good, right, perfect, "make us proud."
(5) Don't be selfish.
(6) Do as I say, not as I do.
(7) It's not okay to play or be playful.
(8) Don't rock the boat.

Picture yourself as a young woman in a family where these eight rules are in place and where you are validated *not* for who you are, rather for who/what the family needs you to be. In a conflict with a loved and valued family member, your genuine feelings are almost impossible to experience. The progression and development of codependence is slow and potent; consequently, when your thoughts, feelings and behaviors have been shaped by fear and compliance, and a quest for some form of approval, conflicts product mostly confusing feelings. Over time your true feelings will not have been validated; thus, when you feel pain, anger or fear, you have difficulty recognizing it, accurately labeling it, or expressing it.

You may feel more than one feeling at the same time. You might think you are angry but fear expressing it because you can't be certain what the anger is about. Maybe you express anger and end up crying. You could be afraid, but unclear if it's justified. As feelings emerge, you struggle to understand what *you* are feeling, what the *other* person is feeling, and what is acceptable to express in the interaction. Most importantly, you become willing to stuff whatever you feel to preserve the relationship—to make the conflict go away.

The issue of acceptability will almost always be important when you have had a family history of dysfunction. The reality of any feeling and its existence is generally secondary to the question of "Is it okay to say what I'm feeling?" The conflict inside creates dysfunctional behavior, a feeling of being stuck, and the general sense of powerlessness. The questions inside are, "What can I do? How can I get through this? What if I ruin everything? What is the best thing for me to do? How can I handle this situation? Will _____ still like (or love) me? Why can't I do things right? What's wrong with me? Maybe I am crazy."

It is usually after the interaction ends, after you are alone and have time to look back and process and think and get in touch with yourself that you know what you should have said, what you could have said, how you could have handled the situation, and even how you might have taken care of yourself. To be in touch with "self" in the middle of a confrontation is extremely difficult unless you have been lucky enough to have been validated for feeling what you genuinely feel. Most women frequently find themselves unable to identify feelings. Being out of touch with feelings usually manifests in dysfunctional thinking—beating yourself up, "I wish I had done something different. I did something that was not good for me. I can't believe that I handled something so poorly. I can't believe I have myself in such a mess. Why am I so incompetent? Why am I so stupid? What's wrong with me, now?"

Dysfunctional thinking keeps you stuck, and being stuck is being powerless. Unfortunately, this is the condition of most women's lives much of the time. You find yourself stuck in emotional states you don't understand and can't handle. You find yourself stuck in life-styles that are unfulfilling and unproductive, in careers or jobs that are meaningless, in interactions in every aspect of life where your needs aren't met. Almost all women speak of being stuck in a state of loneliness with few to no relationships or in relationships that do not give them what they really want or need most.

Codependent Relationships

What is the difference between a healthy adult relationship and a codependent relationship? How does codependency manifest in our adult intimate relationships? What does codependency do to our day-to-day interactions?

A model for healthy, non-codependent relationships can be visualized by creating your own hand puppet show. Hold your hands perfectly straight, palms facing. Each hand represents a healthy non-codependent individual. In a healthy relationship, you see two individuals of either sex and of any age facing each other. Move your palms closer together letting them touch. Notice that as the individuals move together, they are erect and they are firm and solid in their oneness. As they come together to create intimacy, they do so with the ability to make connection at all levels because they are solid in their individual energy and in their approach to one another. Consequently, they connect physically (sometimes sexually), emotionally, intellectually, and spiritually. The contact is deep and satisfying. It is nourishing to the body, mind, emotions, and spirit.

As the individuals move away from each other into their states of autonomy, (separate your palms by two feet—keeping them straight) they maintain their energy, standing straight and strong. They function solidly and with joy and enthusiasm in their worlds of autonomy—their private time, work time, volunteer time, and social time. Then they slowly, gradually, and easily flow back toward their primary relationship and connect once again. (Palms back touching.) Thus, in the healthy relationship, there is an easy flow, a movement into intimacy, a movement away from intimacy into autonomy, a movement back to intimacy , and a movement back to autonomy. In this healthy relationship increased levels of intimacy enhance the individual's ability to be autonomous. Increased levels of autonomy enhance the individual's ability to be more intimate, and further, add to the richness of the intimacy. Intimacy feeds autonomy and autonomy feeds intimacy. Deeper levels of each state are possible to explore. Each creates a sense of personal satisfaction, and is valued for what it is, for being.

In healthy dependency, it is okay to lean, to need, to move toward the other to be taken care of. (Keep one palm straight, bend the other over slightly, allowing finger tips to rest on the straight palm.) The partner nurtures without suffocating and without taking over. This kind of support strengthens the individual to stand back up and once again to rely on self rather than developing a permanent posture of codependent leaning. Then the other partner can feel free to lean, too. The process can repeat over and over, as needed, with the mutual meeting of healthy dependency needs.

In the codependent relationship, one individual has leaned heavily into or onto the other person and the other person has curled over and around the person who is leaning. A codependent relationship model can be visualized by curling one hand into a fist and curling the other over it, protectively controlling and holding. You can see that in this posture of being curled into one another, the same level of touch at all four levels seen in the first example is not possible. The individuals may trade places in this kind of relationship. The opposite person may lean while the other also switches position and curls over and around. This relationship creates a sense of clutching and neediness, and for some people, a claustrophobia, a sense of being trapped. Consequently, it is hard to feel autonomous. Rather than a smooth movement into autonomy, people break away, flee, run away in some manner, from this kind of intimacy. They pull away from each other rapidly and dramatically and rush into some autonomous act or activity. (Wrench your hands apart, separate by two feet, keep curled up in fist.)

Because the individuals have pulled away or run away from the intimacy, the autonomy produces guilt feelings, and for some people, a sense of panic or fear about being "out there" alone. They are still physically, intellectually, emotionally, and spiritually "curled up," so their autonomy is not full or satisfying, and the individuals rush back into, sometimes dash back into, the codependent intimacy.

In a codependent relationship there is an abrupt running toward and a running away from one another. The smooth flow back and forth between autonomy and intimacy, seen in the first example, is lost. Here, full intimacy is never experienced. And true autonomy is never experienced. Because the needs of the individuals are never fully met, each person feels a sense of loss, a lacking, something that is not quite right or not quite what they expected this intimate relationship (or this autonomy) to be.

People who are codependent create this kind of pattern in most, if not all of their individual and group relationships at home and at work. To examine this in your own behavior, simply think of all the relationships that are important to you. Make a list of the ten individuals who are most significant in your life. They can be family members, work associates, close friends, anyone you would like to list. Study the list and by the name of each individual, indicate the following:

(1) Do I think I give more to this person than I get in return?
(2) Do I think I receive more from this person than I give?
(3) Do I perceive the relationship to be a balance of give and get?

If you are highly codependent, you will discover that most of your relationships feel out of balance. You will discover, as you examine your behavior with this individual, that you are the one who does most of the giving. You will discover you get very little from the people around you. As you reach in to retrieve more feelings, you may find you feel hurt by this lack of intimacy. At a level farther down, you may touch feelings of anger. Once you are able to experience the anger, you can be assured that a healthy, although scary, part of your inner self is being activated. The anger, when understood and dealt with in an effective manner, signals integrity. You realize something is wrong, something needs clarification, and change is necessary. These are the first feelings you need to recognize to move from codependence, that ultimate state of powerlessness—back toward reclaiming and owning your own personal worth, your authentic self, your personal power.

Exploring, Questioning, Reflecting

1. Refer back to the eight family rules for dysfunctional or addictive families on page 39. Using a rating scale of 1 through 10 (1 represents not a rule in my situation; 10 represents an intense rule in my situation), rate your family of origin.

2. Using the same scale, rate your current living environment.

3. Finally, rate the organization you work in, own, or do volunteer work for.

4. Go back to the exercise on page 43. List the most significant people in your life if you haven't already done so. Ask the three questions.

   a. Do I think I give more to this person than I get in return?

   b. Do I think I receive more from this person than I give?

   c. Do I perceive the relationship to be a balance of give and get?

5. Reflect on and write about any codependent behaviors you see in yourself.

CHAPTER 4

POWERLESSNESS AND ADDICTIONS

"Defeated attitude. It's a man's world. Something's wrong with me vs. the powerful. Always busy—sidetracked from reflecting on obtaining power and learning/knowing what I want."

"Need more education—constantly. I feel too emotional to confront situations. Overeat, fat people don't control power."

"Lack of self-confidence in self. Unwilling to take a risk."

Powerlessness can manifest in an additional deadly form—addictions. Powerlessness grows in the individual until it is strong enough to be called codependence. A codependent person, untreated, will likely become addicted to some substance or process.

Powerlessness = Codependence = Addictions = Powerlessness

What are the connections between codependence and addictions? Return to the example of the child and the broken bike in

Chapter 3. The child pushes authentic feelings out of her awareness in order to behave in ways to receive parental approval and acceptance. She looks outside herself to identify behavior that "works" and learns to behave codependently. Her real feelings are still present and she must find a way, usually on her own, to deal with authentic pain and fear, and eventually shame.

Most children learn to find a behavior, an activity, or a substance to distract their awareness from their feelings. In the absence of guidelines, teaching, or support from adults in the family, children unconsciously become quite inventive in taking care of their unacceptable feelings. Some examples include:

(1) Learning to be perfect
(2) Working so hard that there is no time to feel
(3) Creating an imaginary world—or imaginary friends—for escape and interior conversation
(4) Watching television endlessly
(5) Excessive reading or studying
(6) Overeating
(7) Excessive physical activities; athletics or physical aggression.
(8) Rebellious or more self-destructive behaviors which at least take away the original pain
(9) Sexual acting out and eventual use of alcohol, drugs, and cigarettes

Whatever the behavior/activity, the individual experiences relief from feelings perceived as unacceptable or unsafe to express. The relief signals the system that the behavior works: "I feel better than I did" (at least for a while). When the feeling of relief subsides, the behavior must be repeated to get the desired sensation again. As the pattern is repeated, the individual learns to associate feeling better with the medicating substance, process, or person. Here we see the beginning of addictive tendencies. When patterns of behavior or use of a substance are repeated time after time, an addiction develops. Real feelings denied grow stronger but are pushed more deeply underground. More and more of the substance or process is needed to keep real feelings "under control." The individual, now addicted to a process or substance, has reached the ultimate state of powerlessness.*

Most of us, unfortunately, have addictions or addictive behavior. Addictions, when seen as powerlessness, are obvious ways to hold ourselves back, to hold on, to deny the authentic self, to not feel who we really are. Addictions are attempts to control feelings rather than feeling them. What are the substances and processes we use to so significantly alter who we are, what we see and feel?

SUBSTANCES to which people become addicted:

alcohol	drugs	food
nicotine	caffeine	sugar

PROCESSES to which people become addicted:

relationships	romance	sex
work	gambling	spending
television	exercise/dieting	fitness/youth
religion	spiritual ideas	negative power
rage	institutions	therapy

It is often difficult for women to relate to the idea of being addicted. For a moment, let go of addiction labeling and simply reflect on these questions:

(1) When you're dissatisfied or feeling unhappy or unsettled, what do you do?

(2) When painful, angry, scared or lonely feelings surface, how do you handle them?

(3) When conflicts emerge in your significant relationships, what do you do? What do you say?

(4) When problems develop at work, how do you approach them? How do you feel?

(5) When you have strong ideas, opinions, wants, needs, and feelings, what do you do?

*See diagram of Development of Addiction in Appendix B.

(6) When those same strong ideas, opinions, etc., are in conflict—or even slightly different from those of the person with whom you're talking, what do you do?

(7) When you're feeling anything, physically or emotionally, that you don't like or don't want to feel, what do you do about it?

As you reflect on these questions, what is your assessment of your responses? The goal is not to get you to admit to addictive behavior. The goal is only to assist you in observing yourself and your behavior. You may, in fact, have no addictive behaviors. But if you do, you deserve to begin to identify and understand them. Doing so is difficult because denial is strong in each of us and our entire society encourages denial and supports addictive behaviors. Denial is redefining, minimizing, rationalizing, explaining away, laughing at serious subjects, and otherwise finding methods to support the behaviors in which we engage which aren't good for us.

Think about the last beer commercial you saw and how everyone drinking was attractive, sexy, happy, and usually young. The real effect of the substance on bodies, minds, experience, and emotions is lied about through omission. Remember again, the last time you stood in the checkout line at the grocery store and casually viewed the cover of a women's magazine. The cover blares out the rewards of the most recent fad diet and/or exercise program and simultaneously shows you a delicious looking chocolate cake. Remember too, the last time one of your children cried for a cereal covered with sugar and salt because she or he has seen so many commercials for it on television. Visualize the last billboard or magazine ad you saw for caffeine or nicotine and the association with happiness, contentment, and successful relationships. Remember the last social or work related conversation you overheard or engaged in where overwork to the point of physical, emotional, and mental exhaustion was praised and validated. Remember the last conversation you tried to have with family members who kept watching television with one eye. Consider the last bad relationship you discussed and cried about with a friend. Last, but not least, remember the adrenaline flow you may have experienced from shopping or gambling or simply spending too much money—money you knew you could not afford to spend.

The things you identify in your mind's eye, the events you are recalling are aspects of individual, family and cultural contradictions and denial about our behavior, our activities and possibly about some of our addictions. The sad reality is that the majority of people in our culture have become addicted to some substance or to some process. The degree of the addiction may vary dramatically, but addiction is present and must be examined at all levels, in private lives and in the world of work.

Self examination is difficult. Most of us are thwarted by the following kinds of thoughts:

- "Maybe if I look at myself, I will find there is nothing there."
- "If you only knew what went on inside me, you couldn't possibly be my friend or like me or love me or want to even acknowledge a relationship with me."
- "If you explored my knowledge about this subject, you would discover that I am really a fraud.
- "I have no idea who I really am."
- "I am terrified of what is really inside me."

These are examples of the beliefs that abound in the minds and hearts of most of us and cause us to back away from looking at our essence as human beings. However, the need to know, the need to be connected with self, and an even greater need to be connected with others, with our community and with our universe, is strong in each of us. The addictive behavior is powerful and delusional and most significantly, a substitute to avoid our essence by giving us an artificial sense of reaching that which we desire.

Initially, the dysfunctional behavior gives the illusion of connectedness. In other words, when you shop with friends, drink with friends, smoke with friends, use with friends or in any way engage in group behavior that has addictive qualities or substances, you may feel that elusive sense of connectedness or belonging. The frightening, eventual reality is that the substance or the process that temporarily makes you feel connected gradually separates you from that feeling of connectedness. As addictions grow stronger you experience more isolation and alienation and your physical, psychological, mental, and spiritual processes diminish. Fear and paranoia intensify. Eventually, this on-going process separates you from what you value most—relationships. The most damaging effect of an addiction is that it separates you even farther from the authentic self.

Exploring, Questioning, Reflecting

1. Return to the beginning of this chapter. Answer the questions on pages 47 and 48 in as much detail as you can.

2. Review the list of addictive substances and processes. Honestly ask yourself if you have become dependent on any substance or process listed. If you are concerned about any of your behaviors and do not know how to get help, consult the resources in Appendix A.

Section II

Techniques for Self-Analysis

Chapter 5

Questions for Getting Started

"If I let all my personal power out, I would feel very self-confident and it would give me a great feeling of well being and being my own person. I'd feel more important to myself particularly."

"I don't know for sure."

"Look out world, Here I go—doing, instead of thinking about it."

A major part of the authentic self that has been lost and must be retrieved is a positive image of being female. In this section, we explore ideas and techniques for reclaiming the self and regaining personal power. A starting point is acknowledging *being* a woman.

Being a woman is special, and in our society today, it is still significantly different from being a man. Early psychological research led us to minimize the differences between women and men. Studies of men were used to predict or understand women's

*See Carol Gilligan, *In a Different Voice;* Mary Belinkey, et al., *Womens Ways of Knowing;* Harriet Lerner, *The Dance of Anger;* Lillian Rubin, *Intimate Strangers;* Anne Wilson Schaef, *Women's Realities.*

behavior—a yardstick that just doesn't work! Carol Gilligan, Mary Belinkey, et. al., Harriet Lerner, Lillian Rubin and Ann Wilson Schaef were some of the first writers to help us identify significant differences. It is only through understanding our differences that women and men can eventually come together. Our differences from men define our uniqueness while the constant comparison to men, using men as the benchmark for health and success and development, has kept us off our own track and confused our processes of growth and development.

Our sociocultural norms support and teach women to view their primary developmental task as the building of significant relationships within a family context. The secondary developmental task is to focus on self and work/tasks. For men, the opposite is true. Their primary developmental tasks are work/tasks and self. Their secondary focus is relationships. Perhaps in a better world, both men and women would be able to attain a balance through accomplishing both the primary and the secondary sets of developmental tasks. However, in our complex, sexist, and patriarchal society, the roles have unfortunately crystallized with a sole acceptable focus for each sex: relationships for women, and work and self for men. Even as we enter the new millennium, moving outside these rigid expectations results in a negative societal response. Psychological group pressure is applied to drive the individual back "inside the lines" and to comply with the traditional expectations. Many women continue to "violate" cultural expectations and to lead lives outside these traditions, but the pressure is still real, and regardless of the degree of our sophistication and liberation, each of us feels the impact.

Perhaps when you hear often enough that you don't fit in with your own sex group because you strive to be yourself, it is a logical response to try to fit in with the other sex group. Thus, many women try to become more like men. We have seen for years that men in general are more successful, have more resources available to them, and appear to have more flexibility and power than women. It has been seductive to try to belong, particularly in the world of work. Additionally, we have been told there is little value in our lives as women; in the way we view the world, the things we hold dear, our approach to relationships, and particularly our ways of functioning in organizations.

Women have been discriminated against. Perhaps even more importantly, our sex as a group has been psychologically and spiritually diminished. Many of us learned at an early age not to associate with other women because they were regarded as scatterbrained, weak and uninteresting. Yes, some of us joined consciousness-raising groups and acknowledged our competition with one another for that most valuable of commodities—the attention of men. We learned to network and help each other, yet, when management literature demonstrated how similar we were to men in our abilities to function in the real world, many of us rejoiced. Only in recent years have we begun to back track and pick up what we lost in our rush into the white male competitive arena— our true selves and our serenity.

Owning our female qualities is valuable for our own growth and development and for the potential contribution to others and to organizations. Owning this value is a part of retrieving the authentic self. In the 70's, Margaret Henning and Ann Jardim* told us that not learning to sacrifice our values around the importance of relationships for the overall benefit of the team, was one significant defect in our ability to function in the world of work. Our socialization was, in fact, a liability. In the 80's, Carol Gilligan** challenged us to reexamine this point. Perhaps our willingness to sacrifice the game in order to maintain the relationships is not so bad after all? Whatever the right answer, it doesn't help to emphasize one approach and eliminate the other. A balance of female-male approaches is needed.

Alice Seargent*** introduced the concept of androgyny into management thought. Androgyny is blending the best of female and male principles. For this to happen, women must begin to know who we are and to believe in what we know and in what we can bring to the failing institutions in our society. We must articulate and value our knowledge if we are to offer it to our families, our schools, our churches, and our organizations.

*The Managerial Woman—Margaret Henning and Ann Jardim
**In a Different Voice—Carol Gilligan
***The Androgynous Manager—Alice Seargent

Many women experience the conflicts raised about their role in our society. The women's movement has made it an issue not to be ignored. Regardless of whether you see yourself as liberated or traditional, the value the culture does *not* place on your being a female affects you. The confusion about acceptable modes for "how to be" is painful. Women in their 40's, 50's and 60's have had very few significant role models for how to be the individuals they are striving to be. This group of women, in general, is more clearly different from their mothers' generation than any preceding generation of mothers and daughters. That means that those of you in your 40's, 50's, 60's and older are pioneers. Whatever kind of life you are leading, chances are it is something you are learning as you go along. It is on-the-job training! If you are struggling to understand who you are as a person and as a woman, in a society that wants you to be something you are not, it can be difficult and painful. Understanding your femaleness is a major part of discovering and reclaiming your authentic self.

Self-System Analysis

Release from powerlessness is complex and it is never easy. The necessary hard work, however, opens the door and creates the pathway for the journey back to the authentic self. This journey is always worth the work.

Each woman has her own starting place and time. There is no right way or perfect beginning, only techniques, philosophies, and theories for guidance. The problems each of us face can sometimes best be understood by looking at the self and sometimes by looking at and understanding the system. There is a "saying" that reminds women to examine the system as a potential source or at least partial source of the problem.

Sometimes the reason you feel crazy is because you're in a crazy situation—not feeling crazy may be the thing that means you really are—and that makes feeling crazy the only possible *sane* response!

Our tendency is to look at ourselves as the source of the difficulty and to wonder, "What have I done wrong?" "What's wrong with me?" We may ask, "How did I blow it this time?" Amazing as it may seem, you are not always the problem or the cause of the problem. The reflex to assume you are is often ingrained. Once, while giving a speech on this very subject to a large convention of women, I became aware that my voice was no longer carrying over the sound system. Immediately I stopped talking to examine my hand mike to see how I had turned it off. My first response was not to say, "The system has failed." It was, rather, to see if I had done something *to* the system. Both were, and always are, possibilities, and it is important to examine both.

Become knowledgeable about *both* yourself and the system in which you are having conflict. Conduct a balanced analysis. Blaming yourself or blaming the system accomplishes nothing, but understanding yourself and the systems in which you live and work builds perspective and the insight needed to feel in charge of your life and your choices. You will probably need to seek out information about the system. Most of us have not been socialized to be savvy in system-analysis.

Today both individual and system issues are confusing. On the individual level, increasing numbers of women have gained visibility in a variety of businesses and professions. Access to higher management positions seems easier. The availability of higher education in all fields has increased. It is hard to argue that things have not changed, because so many women are working in a broad and exciting range of careers. Individual women are succeeding. However, on the system level, the data are more grim. Women are the fastest growing poverty group and group of illiterates in the world. Aging women around the world are alone, homeless, and starving. Women of all ages, classes, and races are beaten, raped, abused and murdered. Women have difficulty collecting child support as well as alimony, and many have difficulty supporting children on single, minimum wage incomes. Millions of women are displaced homemakers.

System problems or the problems of women in the larger system gradually and powerfully impact the life experience of all women. The fear, pain and confusion we face as individuals is heavily intertwined with the confusions and contradictions and the failure of many of our systems.

It is tempting to assume that there is nothing an individual can do to change the conditions of the world or to be more supportive of women. The reality is you can make a difference for yourself and your world. *Act,* today, in any way you can. Examine yourself, identify your problems. Start now and make your life as healthy as possible.

Exploring, Questioning, Reflecting

A list of questions, a "self-system analysis" follows. Try answering the questions, if only with a few words at first. As you move through the questions, you may want to expand your answers. In that case, go back and write more. Use the questions in whatever way you find helpful. Remember, that not knowing the answer to questions is okay. Peeling off the layers of denial and gradually increasing your level of awareness is part of the journey.

SELF-SYSTEM ANALYSIS

1. *SELF*
   Take a long hard look at who you are today—personally and professionally. What do you value most?
   What are your strengths and weaknesses?
   What are your goals and priorities?
   How do you feel about yourself?
   What do you like most about yourself?
   What do you dislike most about yourself?
   What needs to be changed?

2. *ATTITUDES AND BELIEFS*
   What do you believe about being a woman?
   What are your assumptions about life?
   What are your expectations for your life?
   Do you feel like a victim or do you believe you are in charge of your life?

3. *BEHAVIOR*

   Is your behavior congruent with your values, goals, priorities, attitudes, and beliefs?

   Do you find that you say one thing and do another? If so, do you understand this behavior?

   Do you seek contacts and work opportunities with and for other women?

4. *FEEDBACK*

   How do others perceive you?

   Is the feedback you receive positive, negative, inconsistent, or is there an absence of feedback?

   Do you know people whom you trust to ask for information on how you are regarded, both personally and professionally?

   Are you willing to ask for such data, listen to it, evaluate it, use it?

5. *SITUATION*

   What are the specific situations in your life that you find problematic?

   Who are the people involved?

   What is the nature of the interaction, the work to be done?

   When does the conflict or difficulty emerge?

   What resources do you have for confronting the problems?

6. *ENVIRONMENT*

   What is your immediate environment like? What is your family life like?

   Describe your work or volunteer life?

   How would you describe the "climate"? Or if you were taking the temperature, what would it be?

   Do you find that you feel your home or work settings are a crazy place to be?

   Who are the people that make your home or work place seem crazy?

   What kind of work do you do?

How do you or your superiors organize your work?
What is the day like?
How does the day flow?
Do you feel valued as a person and as a professional?

7. *SYSTEMS* (Think of a system that you function in today.)
   How well do you understand the entire system?
   Where are the sources of formal and informal power?
   Who is in charge?
   What are the system's values?
   What is the system's true attitude toward women?
   What resources do you have access to within the
      system?
   Are you using an existing network within the system?
   Could you start a networking group?

These questions are intended as a beginning. As you explore and write your thoughts about these seven areas, you are moving along a continuum from self to system. You will begin to see where and in what areas you need more information.*

---

*When you discover that you are ready for more detailed or more specific questions, refer to *Paths to Power* by Natasha Josefowitz. The appendix in her book provides detailed questionnaires that are specifically geared to work analysis.

CHAPTER 6

WHAT DO I DO NOW

"If I let all my personal power out I'd be the type of person who couldn't be intimidated and would be able to proceed in my professional life and personal life."

"Trust my own inner feelings. Do things that are important to me—more often. Learn to lose weight and maintain a weight I am more comfortable with—NOT necessarily think by others' standards."

"I would feel more self confident and 'sure' of my decisions. OK about if they were right or wrong because they were mine—greater feeling of inner strength and peace."

Once you begin to ask the questions raised in the preceding chapters, you want answers. What do I do? How do I understand more? How can I fix it? The answer: go farther inward, examine deeper levels or layers of the self; and go outward, examine your environment, your society. The pathways are numerous and varied. One approach is never effective for everyone. Exploring metaphors, concepts, and questions that really "jiggle" your awareness helps.

Understand the Contents of the Trash Compactor

By the time a woman reaches her late 20's or early 30's, the trash compactor described earlier is generally full, and the overload light is flashing! The contents are layers of tightly compressed feelings of anger, pain, disappointment, regret, loneliness, fear, and often rage. There are also many unexpressed feelings of love and joy. When there is no immediate relief most women ooze "leaky garbage." They cry easily, usually when watching greeting card commercials on television or when someone says something nice to them. Women who don't cry easily are often tense, testy, irritable, and in male language, bitchy. When these symptoms are experienced, the majority of women try even harder to control what they're feeling. More attempts to control leads to more "holding on." You hold your breath, limiting not just your breathing but your experience, your full and healthy flow of life. As the natural flow of life is limited, illness often develops.

Obviously the contents of the trash compactor need to be understood, then cleaned out. But since control and holding on creates such a tight layering of feelings, understanding is confusing, and often overwhelming. Anger and pain, for example, are often inseparable and you may often feel both at the same time. Just at the moment you intend to express deeply felt anger, you cry instead, much to your frustration and confusion. Now a self-defeating process begins. You are angry with and critical of yourself because you didn't know what you were feeling. You didn't say or do the right thing. You blame yourself and add more negativity to the compactor. The original feelings are still there, still misunderstood.

The key is to feel the feeling without judgment or self-criticism. This is hard to do! However, giving yourself permission to feel whatever is there, whatever comes up, is the beginning. Many of the feelings buried in the compactor are unknown to you on a conscious level and the need to have them surface, to deal with unknown content, can be frightening. Fears, as well as self-criticism, cause the feelings to stay submerged. Risking confronting the unknown through letting go, letting feelings out and accepting them for whatever they are is essential. One common fear is that "If I allow myself to feel, I'll find that there is nothing inside me." Another frequently expressed fear is "If I let myself cry (or get angry), I'll never stop. I'll lose control. I'll go crazy." This is not true.

Often your response to a difficult or conflicting situation surprises you by its intensity. You might think, "Anyone would have been upset/hurt/angry, but why was I *that* upset/hurt/angry?" Your reaction seems out of proportion to the event. When this happens, it is usually an indication that you have been in a situation or interaction that stirred old layers of feeling in the trash compactor. You are reminded (at an emotional or physical level) of another time and place where you felt the same way, or of another person much like the individual with whom you are dealing. The "recall" can be last week, 20 years ago, or both. You might discover numerous situations or people reminiscent of your present dilemma, an emerging pattern.

Think of a long thread running through a complex fabric pattern or a string of pearls or rosary beads. The end you hold in your hand represents the present situation, and as you pull, you see that each section of the cloth or each pearl or bead represents a piece of your past, a scene that can be recalled sometimes with pain and fear. Making these connections, seeing the pattern, is vital to understanding.

Identifying the pattern is also helpful in figuring out what causes intense, overly dramatic reactions. Old feelings held down contain enormous energy—usually negative and powerful. A current difficult situation or conflict is hard enough in and of itself, but when it taps into old feelings buried in the compactor, those feelings stir and loosen. The energy from old unexpressed feelings moves to the surface and *connects* with the present emotional state. The combination produces a reaction of such intensity that you judge your response as an over-reaction, having little to do with the present situation or person. You feel out of control, confused, perhaps a little "crazy." A patient exploration of the feelings buried in the trash compactor can help you give up the self-negating labels and work at undoing the pattern which, at this point, appears to control you.

When feelings seem overly intense and you choose to examine the contents of the trash compactor, ask yourself when you have felt that way before? Consider if you have been in a similar situation in the past. If you are bothered by someone, ask who that person reminds you of. Does the individual remind you of a former spouse, lover, partner, boss, friend, or one of your children, a parent or sibling? Reflect and write anything that comes to mind. Don't censor your thoughts, just get them down. Trust whatever comes to you. As you write, patterns will emerge. Insights from these patterns will help you as you experiment with new ways of behaving, exchanging old, self-defeating styles of living for actions that work. You will find your new behavior reflects the healthy person you are working to become.

Many individuals can understand the trash compactor contents through talking with friends, reading, writing, reflection, and self-analysis. But many women need professional support as well. It is important that you give yourself permission to ask for help when you need it. Working alone with old and scary feelings can be overwhelming. When you experience doubt, call someone. You may consider seeing a therapist, a minister, your physician. Keep in mind that the goal is to take good care of yourself.

Discovering the Inner Child

Inside every adult women is a little girl. She represents your authentic self, and it is possible you know very little about her or that she exists. There are clues to a less than conscious understanding she is there in some of your comments to close friends or family: "I feel like such a child." "You (to an adult) are acting like a two-year-old." "That sounds like something a kid would say." "You look like a baby." We behave in ways and observe behavior in others that are more childlike than adult. Seldom, however, do we fully understand what such behaviors and feelings mean. Clearly we do not know the importance of examining this aspect of self in order to support our healthy growth and development.

Within you are childhood memories stored from every age. The child you can feel inside of you varies in age, mood, and temperament. Sometimes she is healthy, playful, and authentic. Sometimes she is angry, hurt, scared, and manipulative. Regardless of her behavior and feeling state, she is present and real and has a great deal of impact on you and your behavior as an adult.

The little girl inside is the part of you that needs love, understanding, attention, time, information, and ongoing education for her development and decision-making. In essence you need to parent yourself, your "child within" to help her resolve conflicts from childhood. She is the part of you who holds the memories and feelings—good and bad—of growing up. She knows what she needed, but didn't get, to be healthy and happy. Today she knows what she doesn't get from you.

The child "ego state" or the "inner child" is a rich source of information for you as you examine who you really are. But what does all this really mean and why do you need to understand any of it? Often many of your most powerless states—those times when you can't think clearly or make a good decision—come from the blocked and frustrated energy of your childhood. Recall a recent time of conflict, one that has intense energy for you, one that feels upsetting as you remember it. Think about how you felt, what you did, and what you thought. Think about the people involved—at work or at home.

Take your time and reflect. Ask yourself, "when that happened last week, or last month, how old did I feel?" Listen for the age that pops into your mind. If nothing comes to you the first few times you try, just keep at it. Once you identify an age, take a few minutes and remember what was going on in your life at that age. Where were you living? What was the family situation? What were your relationships like? What do you remember about that period of your life in general? What did you feel at that age?

Next return to the original conflict you identified. What similarities do you see in the adult experience and the childhood memories? Sometimes you will discover that your six-year old self was the one who was in charge of your behavior or your conversation, rather than your adult.

Here's an example: A 12-year old girl attempts to argue and disagree with her father. When he tells her what to do, she yells back, "No one is going to tell me what to do!" The girl is defensive, argumentative, aggressive, and usually ineffective. Many such scenes occur with her father—ones where she never wins and is even punished. There is no instruction or help to learn effective expression of anger. No information suggesting anger is a normal feeling if handled appropriately. Frustration stores up in the form of blocked energy. What happens when the 12-year old becomes an adult?

Fast forward: she is in business meetings with older male authority figures where there is disagreement, where tough negotiations are necessary—there is conflict. She loses her temper, becomes aggressive, defensive, and argumentative, never wins and feels confused about her ineffectiveness. The 12-year old, not the adult woman, "goes" to those meetings. A twelve-year old is too young to be in such a meeting. She doesn't have adequate resources or information and the responsibility is scary and overwhelming. But the energy, the old emotions, of the child take over because it is so "familiar"—so similar to the experiences in childhood. The adult problem-solving and decision-making skills are clouded by unresolved feelings from the past. Discovering more about the 12-year-old-child inside and working on healing the old situations/conflicts still influencing her present behavior leads to change.

A gentle, loving, accepting, receptive approach is needed to uncover the inner child. For individuals who grew up in alcoholic or dysfunctional homes, the child is often hurt, frightened, and angry. Healing is necessary. As healing takes place, the natural child emerges. As the inner child heals and develops, you, the adult, live a healthier, more joyful life.

How do you heal this inner child? You heal through loving, nurturing, and mothering her. Consider all the mothering you do that is directed outward to your own children, spouse, partner, lover, significant others, family members, friends, maybe even bosses and employees. Imagine that kind of other-directed mothering taking a u-turn and being directed back to you.

If the parenting you received growing up was not what you needed, that is still the internalized parent you carry in your mind. We tend to parent ourselves in the same way we were parented. Women and men frequently work hard to make corrections in parenting their own children. We try not to repeat the mistakes we believe our parents made. Often we are successful in behaving differently with our children. Unfortunately we don't treat ourselves with the same kindness. The way we were parented is so well-ingrained that we repeat the patterns on ourselves. Consequently, most people need new internal models for self-nurturing. Those models are frequently available to us when we look at how we nurture/parent others.

Discovering and healing the inner child means visualizing her and talking to her. It means learning to play with her. You can begin making contact with your inner child through guided imagery* or by looking at old photograph albums and selecting pictures of yourself as a child that for some reason speak to you. As you review those old photos, pay attention to your eyes. Select as many pictures as you like. Find one or two that really represent your authentic child.

Next, experiment with internal dialogues on paper or in your mind. Construct the kind of conversation you might have with this child if she were sitting next to you or on your lap. Ask her questions and hear answers naturally pop into your mind. Learn to trust this process. You will begin to get a sense of whether or not it is working. It is most effective to talk when you are relaxed. Sit in a quiet place, meditate or relax by focusing on your breathing for five or ten minutes. Then create a visual image of the child and let a conversation begin. As you practice this technique, it will help to record the content or at least summarize it. Remember that children speak simply, often profoundly, and usually to the point. You will hear things that you want to remember. All you are really doing is accessing your inner knowledge—your deepest sense of knowing who you really are, what you feel, and what you need. This authentic knowledge, though buried, is there once you find ways to reach it,**

---

*References for guided imagery are provided in the resource appendix A.
**For further info see *Healing the Child Within*—Charles Whitfied, *Your Inner Child of the Past*—Hugh Misseldine, and *Self Parenting*—John Pollard

Identifying the Committee in Your Head

Confronted with difficult decisions, many of you find you frequently change your mind or believe you don't know what you really want to do. Often this kind of inner conflict comes from codependent reliance on the significant others in your life and concern with *their* preferences; however, just as frequently the confusion comes from lack of awareness of the "committee in your head." This committee is composed of many different sub-personalities operating inside, many different aspects of the self, and internalized parental constructs. You know that you behave differently depending on whether you are at home, at work, with friends or with new acquaintances. These external differences are manifestations of the internal differences, the varied aspects of who you are. It helps to be able to identify these different parts or these "committee members."

Here is a scenario of "committee members" talking in an unorganized and confusing manner. The holiday season is approaching and you are already involved in your internal (and perhaps external) debate about whether or not to visit your family of origin at their home. As you consider the pros and cons, you discover that you change your mind each time you think about it. You want to go. You don't want to go. You want to go briefly. You want a long, relaxed stay. You would rather have them come to your house, but it would be nice to be able to see other family members and friends by going there. It feels good to think about going. It feels terrible to think about going. You will feel guilty if you don't go. The drive/flight would be fun. The drive/flight would be exhausting! On and on the dialogue goes. What is going on? It is not that you are unable to make the most simple decision, although that is what you tell yourself. These up and down, back and forth thoughts come from the mixed emotions represented by the different voices speaking to you from their own personal experiences with holidays at home.

To understand more fully, extend your image of your inner child to include different ages, an adolescent, a teen-ager, then a college student, a young women, a busy mother, a career woman, and any other images that fit for you. All of them go together to make up who you are. All of these aspects of self have a different opinion to express at the "committee meeting." The six-year-old loves holidays at home because relationships were good then (i.e., Daddy didn't drink) and she was the center of attention on holidays. The 12-year-old is ambivalent because she has begun to have problems with her father who tells her what to do and holidays often mean arguments. The 16-year-old hates holidays. The college student likes going home to relax, see old friends, and catch up on sleep. The young woman has begun a life of her own and wants to establish her own traditions. The mother fights with her mother about how to rear children. The career woman has too many obligations over the holidays to be able to leave for more than a couple of days. All of these components of personality have input and a consensus has to be reached. If your family of origin was dramatically dysfunctional or alcoholic, the debate will be more painful and confusing. Knowing where these many points of view come from can provide some measure of sanity, and ease the sense of craziness.

It is important that you, the adult, make the decision. Your six-year-old or your 12-year-old is too young to assume that responsibility. Besides, you have much more information than either of them. Even if things have changed dramatically in your family, either positively or negatively, since you were six, the six-year-old believes it is still the way it was when you were six. You must realize this or you will make a decision based on obsolete data. Decisions made on outdated, irrelevant information are usually a disaster, but many of us go through life making just such decisions. You can correct this process by understanding the "committee" in your head.

As you experiment with this process you may find that you have memory blocks, big chunks of time you can't retrieve. Although all of us lose our ability to recall details, big periods of loss usually signal that the time was scary, painful, abusive, or somehow difficult for you. It is human nature to choose, at a very deep level, not to remember. Our bodies, however, carry the memory.

Sometimes this information is too difficult to deal with on your own. If the questions and ideas throughout the chapter do not provide enough assistance in getting started, remember it is always okay to ask for professional help.

Identifying Your Early Decisions

Early decisions are those numerous decisions you made throughout your childhood. Early decisions form the basis for your thinking, feeling, problem-solving, and decision-making as an adult. How frightening to consider that most of us go around making important decisions in our personal, professional, and volunteer lives based on information and conclusions drawn as children!

An example: A seven-year old eagerly awaits mother's return from the hospital with her new baby brother. Many family members and friends have gathered at the house for a party. When Mom and Dad arrive, the seven-year old is placed in a large chair and allowed to hold the baby. She is the center of attention now, all the adults are watching and smiling. She innocently asks if she can feed the baby and suddenly, all the adults are laughing loudly! She feels immediate embarrassment which gradually moves to a deeper level of humiliation and shame. The adults know something that she does not know and she is frightened by not knowing, by being put in a situation like this. She does not know what to do. She suspects that what they know has something to do with her mother's body. As she allows herself to think, she realizes that her mother is breast-feeding the baby. Now she is even more embarrassed by her own body and its lack of development. No one explains the situation to her. No one attempts to relieve her feelings. She is stuck with handling this herself so she makes a decision. "I will never be put in this kind of situation again. I will never not know. And if I don't know, I will never look like I don't know." The decision brings relief. It is a way of feeling back in control, of knowing what to do to take care of herself. She had an unpleasant, scary experience, assessed the situation, drew conclusions, and made a decision about how to cope and how to feel safe.

In the future, in similar situations where the need to know is important, the same response is likely to be triggered. Each time she uses this approach—"I must know"—the decision to do so will become more deeply ingrained. It will become a driving force, a way of functioning. Eventually, this decision to know all, will become dysfunctional because it has not been reevaluated. As a high school and college student, this young woman made herself physically ill studying too hard, trying to know as much as she possibly could. As a graduate student, she became ill again. As a career woman, she became a more dysfunctional workaholic, pushing herself to the point of physical exhaustion time and time again until she finally discovered the "early decision" that was driving her. She was afraid to put herself in a situation where she did not know the answers.

Another little girl heard her father say over and over to her and other family members. "If you don't like it, you can leave." This sentence became a part of her belief system. It affected her decision making in significant experiences with conflict. As the decision built its energy over the years, she adopted a pattern of dysfunctional behavior in her life. Whenever she grew even mildly uncomfortable with her surroundings, she left. She walked away from good jobs, from good relationships, and she moved to different cities! She was very confused about her impulsive decision-making until she traced the pattern back to the early decision that gave her internal permission to leave rather than stay and work it out.

Obviously, early decisions have a great deal of energy and control in our adult lives. Knowing these early decisions exist is the first step for change. Then you must "assist the child" to make a new decision. Understanding this process is complex. Specific steps are in *Re-Decision Therapy* by Robert and Mary Goulding.

Questions That Need to Be Asked

Assuming these ideas have begun to broaden your awareness, let's shift and ask some specific questions. Remember, you don't have to know the answer.

(1) Can you color outside the lines?
(2) Are you aware that Superwoman finally caught her cloak in the phone booth door?
(3) Can you give up being a victim?
(4) Do you believe you can be in control if you just try harder?

(5) What do you do to keep yourself from being powerful?

(6) What would happen if you let all your power out?

(7) Do you *want* to reclaim your personal power?

Can You Color Outside the Lines?

Coloring outside the lines is letting go and risking. It is taking a leap of faith. It is doing the thing you fear you may not be able to do. It is giving up the safety of continuing to do that which is familiar, that which you already know you do well. No wonder it is so difficult. And no wonder it is so powerful.

If coloring inside the lines is an image that rings true for you, it is probably difficult for you to take risks, to move against the norm or the mainstream. And there is absolutely nothing wrong with being careful, cautious, intentional, and deliberate before acting. The first question is: Do you behave in this way because you choose to or because you are too afraid to function in any other way? A debate about risk versus caution is irrelevant. Just ask yourself if you are stuck in your cautious, unending collection of data before you act. Many of you have experienced this dilemma around the final decision to leave a relationship; to risk being out there alone, again. The delays seem endless as you ask one more question, engage in one more conversation, make sure you know for certain what s/he meant when s/he said____. You worry about your own feelings and whether you are right or wrong. What if you make a mistake and find yourself in a worse situation? In the 70's, Anne Wilson Schaef suggested women are afraid to make mistakes because they fear they *are* mistakes.* And when you are relatively certain you are "right," you feel safer and better armored when you approach conflict. But "right," is an illusion. It keeps you stuck. Action is the way through difficult "stuckness."

Are You Aware that Superwoman Finally Caught Her Cloak in the Phone Booth Door?

Believing you can have it all may be the most certain, fastest way to continue to mire yourself in powerlessness. Doing more, doing

*See Women's Realities by Anne Wilson Schaef

everything, and doing it perfectly is not the answer. Somewhere along the line, Superwoman crept into our lives as a new role model. As we gave up the original, limited, confining traditional roles for women, we got confused. We added things rather than defining or evaluating priorities. How did it happen? As discussed in an earlier chapter, rapidly changing roles and rigid institutions created a gap. Society has not caught up with the changes in the lives of mothers who work outside the home or women who live alone. New services are not yet adequately provided by the culture. Consequently, too many women are pushing beyond reasonable expectations to do more themselves.

It is not unusual for a woman today to expect herself to be all things to all people. This includes: being happily married or coupled, rearing one or two brilliant and lovely children, succeeding in a career, being active in professional organizations, contributing time to volunteer causes, finding time for political activities, cooking beautiful and nourishing dinners for her family, working out daily, taking her vitamins, meditating, having multiple orgasms at least three times a week, and somehow surviving it all. We may laugh at this list and then secretly wonder if we can achieve it with "more discipline."

This kind of constant "doing" takes women in the opposite direction from what is needed. Women need time for relaxation and reflection. They need time to focus, to put energies to work for the self. As you focus on yourself (what you feel, who you are, what you really want out of life), making decisions, setting priorities, and becoming less dependent on external evaluations of what you are doing becomes easier and more rewarding. Wearing so many different hats (and changing in that phone booth on the corner) is a pathway to powerlessness, to increased levels of codependence, and eventually to physical illness and addictions.

Can You Give Up Being a Victim?

Think of the "victim mentality" as a stuck place with just enough fringe benefits to keep you from really being motivated to work your way up and out. The victim or the martyr is a traditionally acceptable role for women. The victim/martyr is misused, mistreated, and ignored. Nothing goes right. She works hard for little reward.

Victims have a great deal of pseudo-power. Other people try to do things for them, tell them they work too hard, sympathize with their difficult lot in life, offer countless suggestions, and consequently shower a great deal of attention on them. So, if you become the victim, you get some sense of having many of your needs met. The attention is superficially satisfying. Shifting out of a victim position means taking responsibility for what you are doing and feeling. It means acting rather than passively waiting for things to get better. Being a victim is a contract you make with yourself to get by living half a life. Because you don't know what else is out there, being a victim looks better than nothing or the unknown. Each individual must see the unknown as worth moving toward in order to risk the process of letting go. Letting go is one of the most difficult things to do.

Do You Believe You Can Be in Control If You Just Try Harder?

Most of us accept the need to be in control as an acceptable goal. But what is control? It is the opposite of what we strive for in the journey back to the authentic self. Control is holding on. Physically, it is a tightening of the muscles and a constriction of the breath. Emotionally, it is censoring and stuffing. Behaviorally and intellectually, it stops the flow of action and ideas. Spiritually, it is an attachment to the external. Besides all these negatives, control is an illusion. Unfortunately, it is an illusion in which most of our society and our world believes. We form our institutions, from the family to the corporation, with top-down authority. We establish hierarchies, believing that control resides at the top, that the higher up we get, the more control we will have. It is all a myth. Control does not exist. Authority does. Authority resides inside you, the individual. Your internal authority is your personal power.

Try exchanging your need to be in control for a goal of being in charge. Being in charge is breathing and letting go. It is being aware and open and growing and unrestricted. It is a position of making choices and making decisions, a blend of initiating and receiving, all from a state of awareness of what you think, feel, want and need. It is creating your own environment. It is exercising personal power. The transition from being in control to being in charge is a difficult one, possible one step and one day at a time.

What Do You Do to Keep Yourself from Being Powerful?

Common questions I hear from women are, "How can I become more powerful?" "What behaviors must I change?" "What skills must I acquire?" "What contacts should I make to be powerful?" A different approach is to ask, "How do I keep myself from being powerful?" This question is intended to direct you to examine the power you already have, or have the potential for, but for many reasons do not use.

At this time in your life, what are the attitudes, beliefs, feelings, and behaviors that keep you from being as powerful as you are capable of being? How do you diffuse yourself? How do you hold yourself down or back? Try making a list of anything that comes to you. Do not censor it. Just let the ideas flow. Here are some examples to trigger your thinking: maybe you are afraid, maybe you get sick frequently, sleep too much, don't explore options fully, or don't follow through.

The following are responses to the questions from business/professional women from across the country.* As you read, see if any of the thoughts and feelings are similar to yours.

> "Personally, in situations when I feel powerless I have extended myself to serve or satisfy someone else's needs, wants or desires to a degree that I have lost my personal power and am not in control of myself anymore because all of my energy has been spent making someone else happy and I have no time set aside or energy left to spend on 'me'."

*Data collected in seminars conducted by Kay Barnes and Linda Moore.

"Shy away from conflict because of equating success with personal calmness in life-style and tranquility of spirit."

"By giving in or attempting to avoid conflict. 1.) Was raised to believe conflict was bad. 2.) Insecurity 3.) Avoidance.

"I am somewhat like the 'horse' in *Animal Farm*.' If I just work a little harder, everything will be OK. I know that is crazy and have been correcting this attitude—sometimes I'm successful, but when I get into a pinch I feel myself slipping back into that mode. The white Protestant 'work ethic' is strongly ingrained in me and I don't always feel worthwhile if I am not working harder than others, especially harder than men."

"In order not to 'rock the boat' or shake your security we do not step out and assert ourselves. Security. Subject myself (knowingly to my husband's and associates' feelings)."

"I keep myself from being powerful by having to constantly prove myself in a male dominated field."

"By not liking myself."

"I set restrictions on myself that I'm not supposed to be in a position of power. Often, I feel sorry for myself if things don't go well, whether I had control over the situation or not. In attempting to assert myself, I often come on too strong and alienate those around in power positions."

"Difficulty in dealing with conflict or unpleasant situations. Lack of self-confidence causes me to spend a lot of time worrying about others' perceptions of me. I do the things I want to or think I should and then worry about the repercussions of the act in other people's eyes—I judge myself by other people's standards."

"Self-doubt. Women shouldn't be professionals or compete. I'm a woman in a man's field. Need for love and relationships. Play dumb and flighty."

"Afraid to offend others, family as well as co-workers. Trying to please all—all of the time. Easier to take care of everything myself than assert power to urge others to take over."

"Constantly 'giving in' to the decisions of people I perceive to be more powerful; not giving myself the credit/self-confidence in order to create power for myself. Behavior—not being assertive, creating self frustration, generating negative energy, lack of accomplishment."

"I keep myself from being powerful by believing I lack the ability to obtain necessary skills. I fear failure and feel inadequate. My behavior reflects my beliefs about myself. I don't work on skills I feel I need to develop."

"Remain quiet and keep your attitudes, thoughts and ideas to yourself."

"Being afraid of causing problems."

"I feel I will 'check' my behavior and stop myself by my attitude that it is wrong to be powerful."

"Really, a lack of behavior, a lack of skill in knowing how to behave in all situations. Lack of practice. I still have a tendency to become angry in power situations and that makes me powerless. Life should be fair."

"Trained to be just a wife and mother. Inadequate. Down on myself when I don't get the attention of staff or others."

"Saying and doing things that show I can't handle something. Wanting someone to do it for me! Saying—I can't handle it."

"I was raised to believe that the male was the dominating sex and through the years I have been unable to adjust my attitudes and feelings to build my confidence to gain power."

"Belief nurtured by the way we were raised. Feeling that I'm not worthy of power. Difficulty in changing roles. Chauvinism of men in the office keeps me from changing behavior. Feelings stemmed by having excessive inferiority complex when young."

"A behavior of being childish or acting in a submissive behavior. A victim stance. I feel tired or make up illness to avoid power. Primarily migraines."

"Not able to fight enough to demand what I deserve. I feel held back by the emotional stress of such confrontation. I let moral considerations prevent me from taking the power when it is right there to take."

I am an introvert, afraid of being embarrassed in front of others. I fear making a mistake—I'd rather say nothing than be wrong. I have trouble accepting power and all its connotations. The stereotype woman is too big in my mind."

"I guess I'm afraid of what the feeling of power could do to me. On many occasions I have had power and I tend to be dogmatic and unyielding—do it my way or else. I have tempered this somewhat in the last couple of years and am trying to learn the right way. I seem to get in my own way! I know when I have the power when it happens, but don't know how to use it or deal with it."

"I keep myself from being powerful by still wanting my husband to take care of me at times. Although I am the one who does most of the 'taking care of', I rely greatly on him to do the money management. I am emotional about my job, though I have grown tremendously in the last 5 years."

"You can keep yourself from being powerful by failing to educate yourself. A fear of expressing an opinion or idea to a boss or superior can also keep you from being powerful."

"I undervalue my work—I may work hard on a project, a difficult project, in a work situation, but once it's done, I pretend or tell others that the work involved was minimal, and that anyone could have done it and done it better. I don't go after the things I want as aggressively as I see the men around me. I expect others to recognize my abilities by 'osmosis'."

"I keep myself from being powerful by thinking of my faults. It keeps me down and prevents me from reaching towards my goals. I ask myself if my desire for power is mainly a myth. If I really don't want to stay home and be comfortable. Yet, there's a prickling of discomfort if I don't reach for power."

"Fear of being unacceptable to others. Unwillingness to let go of a good relationship. Power does not equate with being feminine. Too much pressure to be powerful/ against personal."

"I worry that I will hurt someone's feelings. I want to be liked. Sometimes people don't respect everyone they like. I fall into 'role' playing with the men I come into contact with—my boss I treat like a 'daddy', my husband as a 'lover'. I hide my power from them."

"Fear of the unknown mostly. Conservative upbringing (which did not encourage imagination and creativity)."

"I believe other women sabotage women who succeed, I don't trust them."

What Would Happen If You Let All Your Power Out?

This question further assumes that you have power but are not using it because of certain limiting beliefs, attitudes or fears. It suggests that you may be holding onto or holding back your power. It suggests that it is possible to release your power. Again, write down whatever comes to you and then check your responses with those of other women.

> "I would have a really shocked and, at least temporarily, angry husband. My children would be relieved because at long last they would not be the only people I used my powers on. My mother, who is also my boss, would probably be irreversibly stunned as she is a very overpowering influence in my life."

> "No one would 'like' me. Boy, would I get things done. Why is 'being liked' so difficult to get rid of—it's keeping me leashed!"

> "Get fired. Be looked down on by other women. Lose my boyfriend. Lose my girlfriends. Laughed at. Nobody would listen to me."

> "Others (men, bosses), would sit up and take notice, not know how to react but have to make the adjustment! It would be OK—would finally be accepted as such— positive, not negative! I would feel better about myself and probably accomplish more. (I'm working on it.)"

> "I would be the person I really want to be—others may not find me OK, but I would!!"

> "I would be over-aggressive, strong and useful. Not liked as well by everyone."

"My husband would not remain and I'd be forced with self support—would be at a lower level."

"I would probably have a nervous breakdown. I have never had the experience of being allowed to express myself to the fullest and I think it would be a frightening experience at the time; but, one that could be looked upon later as a great learning experience."

"I feel that I would achieve all of my goals. In asserting all my power, those that I have tried to keep on an even keel would end up drifting from me. Maybe this would cause me loneliness. Then what good is power if there is no one to share it with—men or women. Overall, I think I'm probably my worst enemy. I often try to overcome this and be my best friend but it is not always easy."

"I would be a forceful yet gentle demanding person in total control of myself and most persons I would be around."

"I believe I would change the lives of all the people around me. Some in a positive way and some in a negative way."

"I would probably have to leave home, and find another position, but I think I would feel great."

"I would probably become very successful—but lonely."

"It would play havoc with my firm, destroy my husband, and kill my kids."

"If I let all my personal power out I'd be 'successful' in a number of ways—personal I mean (not materially). A real sense of accomplishment!!!"

"I would be happier because I would be doing the things I really wanted to do and felt were worthwhile doing. I would be more comfortable relating to other people."

"The positive outcome would be that I could attend staff meetings and voice my ideas about different projects rather than just silently taking notes. Sometimes this 'secretarial' role is incredibly frustrating, especially when the chairperson is a nit-wit who does not encourage participation from the other staff members."

"If I let all my personal power out I could lose love (approval)."

"It would be dazzling but undirected. I'd feel great!"

"I could become angry—I could become demanding. I would get things accomplished and right. I would speak up!"

"I would lose my friends."

"If I let all my personal power out, I would go to the top. I would be happy and feel fulfilled because I had accomplished my major goal."

"Could make better decisions. Better utilization of time. Eliminate useless worry."

"I would be a happier more productive individual, and I feel everyone around me would benefit."

"Feel better about myself. Lose friends and alienate people. (I guess they were not friends after all.)"

"Would make several men highly discomforted. Create—generate anger in others."

"Some would stop in their tracks with surprise. Many objectives could be accomplished without so much hassle. A few may be temporarily offended. I would feel good within."

"Lose friends and lovers."

"I could be anything I wanted to be and do anything I wanted to do. Even become President of the U.S. if I wanted. (And still be feminine.)"

"Nothing. I would be the master of myself and be able to see others as they really are just human beings like myself."

"Break up of a marriage. I would lose my job."

"Would be that my self-esteem would be at its best. Would be rejection from some people I love."

"My family, church, my hometown, my job would be turned around and straightened up fast. A vast improvement as long as I stay true to myself."

"Loss of job. Divorce. Loss of friends (so called)."

"I could do anything."

Do You Want to Reclaim Your Personal Power?

When giving away personal power has been a lifelong process, making a decision to shift gears and to behave differently is no small thing. The reality is that anything you learned to give away you can also learn to get back. A decision to at least begin to take back your personal power means you are willing to make a major shift in all your relationships. With your personal power intact, you behave quite differently. When such a decision is made, a strategy must be clearly thought through. You will create a shift in the "balance of power." The individual(s) to whom you have given power have grown accustomed to having it. You are now expecting them to give it up, and they will not do so easily. In fact, you can expect that the change will make them uncomfortable, scared, and angry!

Consider carefully the relationships in your life that need changing, both at home and at work. Consider making a start with one of those relationships. We have given our power away to many people in both obvious and subtle ways. Choose your own beginning point and if you feel doubtful, know you are in good company. The success of your journey depends on your knowledge of positive uses of power, employing this knowledge, and letting go of old behaviors you have used to gain pseudo power. Chapter 7 outlines positive tools for a new starting place.

Exploring, Questioning, Reflecting

1. Learn to use these questions:
   a. When have I felt this way before?
   b. When have I been in a similar situation?
   c. Who does this person remind me of?
   d. How old do I feel?

   Ask the questions when you are feeling stressed or confused about your reactions and write whatever comes to you.

2. Reflect on the questions, ideas, and metaphors that had meaning for you as you read. For more insight, write, write, write!

3. Once you find a photograph that clearly feels like your inner child, consider these suggestions. Carry a copy in your wallet. Frame a copy for placement in your home or office.

4. Construct a dialogue with your inner child—on paper or out loud—whenever you feel little, scared, inadequate, or in over your head. Reassure yourself in order to regain your center.

5. Review the list of people who have too much power in your life. See if you are ready to experiment with writing about changes you could make in one of these relationships.

6. Make a list of the names of people with whom you have conflicts. Review the list and identify the ways in which these individuals are similar. The similarity can be in behavior, body language or facial expressions, voice tone, style of communication, or beliefs and attitudes. Finally see if these individuals remind you of anyone in your family of origin.

7. Make a list of the kinds of situations or life experiences that are difficult or upsetting for you. Again, look for similarities. Check backwards, through the years, and look for more similar experiences or reactions. You are looking for patterns, and the roots of your feelings may go as far back as your family of origin and your growing up years.

CHAPTER 7

POSITIVE USES OF POWER

"If I let my power out I would be in control of my life."

"Depending on the approach you could destroy relationships."

"Oh, the walls that would tumble! The attitudes would change—my own and others. What a delicious thought!"

Unequal power, in relationships between two individuals or between an individual and a larger group (i.e., the family) or an organization (i.e., the corporation, school or church), generates behavior that is intended to balance the power. People strive to "get even," "get the upper hand," "get back in control," "gain an advantage," "turn the situation around," "get what's coming to them." There is inequality in the balance of power in most of our relationships most of the time, and the amount of power you have or do not have is a significant factor in determining behavior. In other words, you are always doing something to gain a sense of balance, even if it is ineffective or manipulative.

Think about an important relationship at home or at work. If the power is unequal or out of balance, it generally means you do not get what you want or need. When wants and needs are not met you eventually experience dissatisfaction. Your level of care, honor, and investment gradually diminishes.

You feel less involved or less identified as the spouse, the partner, the participant or the employee and you can become apathetic and withdrawn, perhaps depressed. You may instead feel angry and resentful and behave in ways that seem inappropriate to you. Finally you may reject the relationship, organization or activity. Unequal power creates friction, discord, stress, subcultures and "movements"—the women's movement; the counter culture; organizations for the rights of minorities and gays and lesbians; alternative organizations; informal power structures; and the failure of existing organizations.

Continued denial of your dissatisfaction with the imbalance of power, or simply not knowing what to "name" what you're experiencing, exacerbates the confusion and stress in the relationship. Assuming you learned almost nothing about positive uses of power, you find other ways to get what you want—to survive. From childhood as you practice negative uses of power, the development of positive uses of power is interrupted. A set of developmental tasks is skipped. Since negative uses of power can, in fact, get results—even though they damage relationships—the tools needed to use power effectively and positively are not developed.

We begin to understand the positive uses of power by identifying them, defining them, and gradually practicing and incorporating them into our life-styles and our behaviors.

Assertiveness

Acquiring assertive skills is the foundation for developing positive power tools. To be assertive means that (1) you are in touch with what you feel, think, believe, prefer, want, and need; (2) that you are able to express all of these things to the person to whom you are talking (or if you don't, it is a choice not to); (3) that you are able to express these things with an acknowledgment of the feelings, thoughts, and beliefs of the person with whom you are interacting, without putting that person down or negating the difference s/he has with you, and (4) that you are able to act.

Assertiveness skills will either polish and improve your existing abilities in communicating with others or they will help you shift your patterns of interacting in a way that will make a remarkable difference in your life. As you explore the specific tools for becoming more assertive, you will discover there are areas in your life where you are, indeed, successfully assertive, and some areas where you almost never say what you want to say.

At its most basic level, assertiveness means putting yourself first. This is a complex process for women because we have been taught *not* to put ourself first. To shift gears, and to give yourself permission to be first is a wrenching process internally. It is easy to hear how good it will make you feel. It is easy to read about the tools and techniques. It is difficult to implement in your life and in your behavior. At the same time, it is the most basic and important set of tools that you have to develop. Assertiveness provides movement in the direction of creating a personal power base and/or taking back personal power.*

Negotiation

The skills for negotiating follow the development of skills in assertiveness. Many women never reach the negotiation stage because they are either out of touch with what it is they feel and want, or they do not have internal permission to express it. Reaching the stage of negotiation means that your feelings, needs, wants, and beliefs are accessible to you and you are in a position to be able to express them. It means that you are "head-to-head" with the person with whom you are dealing. It means that even though you disagree with the person with whom you are talking, you are in a position to say so, to feel good about saying so, to hear the differences between you, and to negotiate to a position where both people get at least part of their needs met.

It is important to emphasize once more that negotiation cannot take place if you do not know what you want. You also need to know whether or not you are ready to engage in a partial or intense conflict as a result of expressing what you want.

*To explore further, read *The Assertive Woman* by Stanlee Phelps and Nancy Austin.

In negotiation you need to be prepared for resistance from the other person—*and within yourself.*

The process of negotiation begins with (1) defining the problem, (2) deciding what you want, (3) knowing your thoughts, feelings and preferences; (4) speaking your agenda clearly, thoughtfully, directly; (5) *listening carefully* to the thoughts, feelings, and preferences of the other individual; (6) clarifying differences and conflicts; and moving to an agreed upon outcome. The more specific tactics, styles, and techniques of negotiation can be learned either through a workshop or through reading a book on negotiation skills.*

Conflict Management

Conflict management goes hand-in-hand with negotiation and assertiveness. The development of these three tools makes a powerful package for you as you begin enhancing your personal power or taking it back. Conflict management is difficult for women because, as noted earlier, conflict is one of the things women have been taught to avoid. Conflict management means handling differences that emerge between and among people regardless of the level of intensity of the difference. To be a powerful person, you need to be willing to deal with conflictual situations as they arise, regardless of their intensity. Conflict is a part of personal power. Conflict can be something simple like a mild difference between you and another person. It can also be an intense, painful, scary argument. Conflict management means facing these varying degrees of differences. It means confronting them, dealing with them and working them through. Imagine that you are chairing a committee where members are outspoken, argumentative, and disagree with one another. In this case your task is to manage differences and conflicts and facilitate the development of a group product.

Facing your fear of conflict is essential. Your internal sense of comfort with conflict will come over weeks and weeks of practice. Don't expect it to feel comfortable immediately. The skills

---

*Pursue this concept through reading *Winning by Negotiation* by Tesa Albert Warschau.

needed, once again, can be acquired through practice and by reading a variety of books on the subject or attending workshops in your community.

Goal Setting

Goal setting is one of the most important positive uses of power; however, if you've read extensively and gone to dozens of workshops it may sound old and overdone to you. Regardless, the key to goal setting is to focus on understanding what it is you are striving for, what it is you want, what it is you need, and to begin to write it down and say it out loud. Goals take on a new energy once they are put in writing or are spoken aloud.

If you are confused about your goals, begin to write down the things you think you want for your life. Through goal setting you are making a commitment to yourself to take responsibility for your life. Remember that spoken and written goals are not set in concrete. Goals, like rules, are made to be broken. They must be reevaluated on an ongoing basis, redefined when appropriate, and changed altogether when necessary. Goals "get your motor humming" but they don't restrict and limit the direction you drive. Two guides for goal setting are to change them as you change and always write them down.

Establishing Priorities

Once you are able to establish goals, it is important to learn to set priorities. When goal setting is difficult, being able to set priorities can seem impossible. However, setting priorities is essential because it helps you focus the direction of your energy.

Establishing priorities gently nudges you in the direction of being honest and straightforward, at least with yourself, about what is most important to you. The process also assists you in using your time wisely. Sometimes a priority-setting exercise helps you see your level of confusion and internal contradiction; you have trouble deciding which goal comes first, second, or third. The priority setting process guides you toward being responsible to yourself. Try this: list the ten most important things in your life. Put each on a single slip of paper. Now if you had to give one up, which would it be? Now, two—and continue until you know the order of your preferences.

Visualization

Once you have established priorities for your goals, it's time to act. Visualization facilitates action. Begin by creating, as clearly as possible, a visual image of your goal. If you have initial difficulty creating pictures in your mind, leaf through magazines until you see images that reflect your ideas. The key is to create a clear, detailed image in your mind of what you are working toward. The combination of visualization techniques and goal and priority setting becomes, again, another set of powerful tools. The field of visual/guided imagery while new, is potent and useful to anyone who chooses to develop this skill.

In a state of relaxation (induced either by meditation or by closing your eyes, doing deep breathing, and letting your whole system relax) you can create a detailed image of what you are working toward. You see the situation as clearly as possible. You see yourself going through all the motions of accomplishing whatever you are working toward. This goal may be to become president of a corporation. It may be to take off 25 pounds, to improve your tennis serve, or to have a constructive and useful interaction with your mother. It is more likely your goal will be achieved when you take the time to visualize—when you are able to see yourself successfully moving in the direction you desire.

Affirmations

As you can clearly visualize yourself accomplishing a goal, affirmations then become a tool. An affirmation is a positive statement made to yourself about yourself. An example of an all-purpose affirmation is as follows: "I, (your name), like myself unconditionally." Using affirmations means taking a sentence, such as the one above, and repeating it over and over. This repetition can be said silently in your mind or verbally said out loud. You can record the affirmation on a tape recorder and listen to it over and over. It is also effective to write the affirmation over and over.

Affirmations do two important things. First, they put new, sensitive information into your "computer." Second they identify the negative thoughts, sentences, and beliefs from your old computer programs.

For example, say the affirmation: "I, (your name), like myself unconditionally." Say it out loud. Now listen and hear the little voice that will issue a disclaimer in your mind. All of us have disclaimers and it's critical that you know yours. A disclaimer is a part of your belief system about yourself. It can control or negatively affect your behavior and your life decisions. Understanding the negative sentences, the disclaimers, that roam around inside your head is the first step in eliminating them. Once you have them on paper, you can confront the negatives and replace them with your affirmations. Many professionals believe affirmations are more effective when repeated in an altered state of consciousness, such as during meditation or during rigorous exercise. Try them while relaxed and meditating, at the end of a meditation, or while exercising.

The connection between affirmations, visualization, establishing priorities, and goal setting may seem obvious to you at this point. Combining all these tools increases the likelihood that you will get your wants and needs met. Combining the use of these tools becomes a powerful part of your efforts to reclaim and enhance your power.*

Time Management

Time management is a positive use of power. Giving away time is a typical female behavior. Thus, learning ways not to give away time is essential. When you give away time, you give away power. Vital energy is lost. Learn not only to manage your time, but also to guard it and value it, and use it in ways that you choose.

Analyze and evaluate the way you use your time. Read about time management or go to a workshop. Taking charge of your time is simply another way of taking charge of your life. When your time is your own, you have begun a process of taking back your power.**

*Pursue through reading *I Deserve Love* by Sandra Ray.
**Pursue through reading *About Time* by Kay Cronkite Waldo and Alex McKenzie.

Delegating

Delegating is certainly a positive use of power and it is closely related to time management. Learning to assign tasks to others and to give up "control" can be difficult. Many women suffer from the "I'd rather do it myself" syndrome. You may frequently decide that if you want something done "right," you must do it yourself. Such an attitude guarantees a misuse of time.

Learn to delegate. Learn to let go, to let others do something for you. Check to see if you assign *tasks* to other people and retain the *responsibility.* An example from home illustrates: One member of your household volunteers to cook dinner two nights a week. You feel relieved of the burden of this activity. However, as time goes by, you discover the only thing the person is doing is the actual *task* of preparing the meal. You have retained the *responsibility* for shopping for the groceries, making sure certain food is out of the freezer in the morning, and doing the preparation for the individual to cook the food. What this means is that you have delegated only the task and retained the responsibility. If this is the case, you indeed may as well keep the task, too. Giving up, letting go of the whole thing, may feel uncomfortable at first But, it's the road to freedom. Delegating at home or at work is essential for you in order to own your power.

Networking/Building a Power Base

Networking is the way women are learning (and need to continue learning) to exercise power as a group. Women's networks are a new experience for us because they have to do with women supporting and mentoring one another. Women being supportive to one another is not new, To mentor or be mentored by another woman, to use the information contacts and connections other women can provide is a major difference. Most of our lives we have asked for support from other women to accomplish something for someone else, or for some worthwhile cause. Today networks emphasize women helping each other for the benefit of one another.

A network is a way to expand your power base. Networks are, at this point, a temporary substitute for institutional recognition of the changing roles of women. Since our institutions define us as powerless, we receive little to no validation in our interactions with our organizations, our schools, and our churches. Networks provide needed feedback and validation from other women.

Networks can be internal or external to an organization. Networks can be composed of women who come from the same profession, or volunteer organization or they may cross all professional and organizational boundaries, expanding into your community. Do not hesitate to seek out a group of women to support and assist in the process of building on or expanding your power base, and gradually learn to network with men.*

Self-Nurturing

Self-nurturing is a process of learning to mother yourself. In these days of tremendous individual and system stress each woman needs to make taking care of herself a priority. It is a powerful tool.

Most women have little experience with self-nurturing. Our socialization teaches us to give that energy to others. We seldom take the time for ourself unless it is "left over." When you constantly give to others, without nurturing yourself, you deplete your own resources. Eventually, you will resent the giving process as well as the person to whom you are giving.

When you give time to yourself, you multiply your energy level and you increase your ability and your willingness to do the things you want and need to do for the other individuals in your life.

For those of you unfamiliar with the concept of self-nurturing, begin this process by making a list of at least 25 things you love to do. Make copies of the list and put them everywhere—on your refrigerator, in your desk drawer, over a mirror, anywhere that you are likely to see it. Then when you are feeling low or just at loose ends, look at your list and read some of the things that make you feel good, rested, and replenished. Give yourself permission to act on those things.

---

*Pursue through reading *Networking* by Mary Scott Welsh.

Exploring, Questioning, Reflecting

1. Select one positive use of power you want to begin working on. If you haven't already worked on assertiveness, that's the best starting place. Choose a book or activity that I have suggested.

2. List the positive uses of power in terms of their importance to you. Then gradually work your way through the list, reading and practicing and, finally, incorporating them into your behavior. Take your time.

3. Try this three step technique when you need to confront someone:
   a. Describe the situation—objectively—as you see it.
   b. State how you feel about it.
   c. State or ask for what you need/want. It's hard, but it makes the interaction more clear to you and the other person.

CHAPTER 8

LETTING GO AND TAKING CHARGE: STEPS TO RELEASE

"I would remove most of the things I felt were barriers and go full speed ahead. My fears and nervousness would be put aside, and I would live each day to its fullest."

"I would immediately realize my ultimate goal in life, being able to express my feelings and opinions without fear and without letting my attitude intimidate me."

"Probably would improve relationship. Provide hurtful self and relationship evaluation. I would move further up more quickly. Co-workers would feel intimidated and threatened, I would have to change my attitudes about my role."

Taking back your personal power and finding your authentic self is a long but exciting process. Uncovering the layers of codependence, confronting the powerlessness that may have come to pervade your life, and developing, nurturing, and maintaining the authentic self is part of your lifelong journey.

A great deal of hard work is seldom appealing, and the suggestion that it might be lifelong or on-going sounds horrendous to most of us! But we have grown up in a world that promises instant gratification and immediate relief from pain and discomfort. We may even have come to believe that we should not have any bad feelings at all.

Many professionals try to convince us that this one book, this particular therapeutic technique, this special spiritual path will fix us. The idea of a quick and permanent fix is indeed seductive. Problems become overwhelming and the processes for confronting them take work. It is tempting to either look for the easy way out or to quit: to quit reading, working, caring. Many women have reached the stuck place of quitting, operating on automatic pilot. You might feel numb much of the time. You may believe there is "too much" to cope with and simply quit trying. This is a dangerous and powerless place. Even if you feel only mildly overwhelmed, and only once in a while, it is important to have some basic thought of what to do and where to start to get release from powerless feelings.

The following specific steps to release come from a holistic perspective, incorporating your physical, emotional, intellectual, and spiritual well-being. Taking back your personal power means looking at all aspects of the self. There are three things that will change your life if done regularly and consistently.

(1) Daily meditation or relaxation exercises.
(2) Regular and rigorous exercise.
(3) A healthy eating plan.

Daily mediation or relaxation exercises are important because they build solitude. Each of us needs time alone to quiet our mind and listen to our inner voice. The daily routines of most women do not include private time alone. This single reality plays an important part in not knowing the self. You must be alone and be quiet to think, reflect, feel your feelings, and to acquaint yourself with your inner voice and your inner knowing. Sometimes "busyness" is intended to keep you from hearing what you need to hear because you fear the answer and the information. Experiment with allowing time for you. Even when it appears totally unrealistic to find time for yourself, examine your options. See if you can alter your daily routine even a little. You deserve it, and it will make a difference in how you feel.

The best time for meditating is first thing in the morning, before you begin your day. It gives you a head start on the morning. You can center and quiet yourself before a hectic tone threatens to take over. The goal is to be quiet and notice what you are thinking, feeling, and how your body is functioning, and to make contact with your "higher self." Sit in a chair with your feet flat on the floor, legs and arms uncrossed, close your eyes, focus on your breath, and gradually let yourself relax and go inward. At first, you are merely getting accustomed to sitting quietly. The ideal amount of time for a meditation is 20 minutes. If it sounds overwhelming to be quiet that long, try 10 minutes. As you become comfortable with the silence try specific meditation or relaxation techniques. References and suggestions for a wide variety of approaches are provided in appendix A.

Regular and rigorous exercise means an activity that accelerates the heart rate, one to work the cardiovascular system. Examples are fast walking, running, swimming, and bicycling. To get the full benefit, the exercise must be done for a minimum of 30 minutes (ideally 40) four to five times a week. It is important not to exercise every day. The body needs time to rest, too. Remember, if you have not exercised for years and particularly if you are over 30, get a check-up from your physician before beginning any kind of exercise program.

The easiest way to start is to pick something that appeals to you and fits your life style. One suggestion is to walk fifteen minutes a day at a pace that does not stress your body. Then gradually build your time and speed until you know you have accelerated your heart rate. Check Dr. Kenneth Cooper's book, *The Aerobics Program for Total Well-Being* to determine your ideal heart rate for your exercise program. Primarily, rigorous exercise aids in reducing stress. A good walk or run or swim is like flushing out your body. Working the muscles frees and releases them. Additionally, rigorous exercise can produce an altered or nonordinary state of consciousness. It rests and enlivens the mind and the body. The body often gives you the first symptoms/signs that things are not okay, that the trash compactor is overloaded; consequently, taking care of and listening to the body is a good starting place for self-nurturing. When your body is working well, you have energy for other areas of your life.

As you meditate, exercise and become more aware, you can begin to pay attention to what you put into your body. The next step is to develop a healthy eating plan, consisting of three well-balanced meals of reasonable proportion a day. A healthy eating plan includes fresh fruits and vegetables, whole grains, legumes, rice, pasta, fresh fish, chicken, and occasionally eggs and lean red meat. It means eliminating caffeine and drastically lowering your intake of sugar, salt, fat and alcohol. You will want to carefully read labels and start reducing and gradually eliminating processed foods and "chemicals."

Standard recommendations for a healthy balance of complex carbohydrates, protein and fat vary with each new diet book; regardless, our more typical American diet, influenced by the amount of processed and fast food we eat, has an alarmingly high percentage of fat and simple carbohydrate intake. Most research suggests that fat and simple carbohydrates must be reduced for long-term health. It is best to check with your physician for the best balance for you.

Why the emphasis on food? You need to put the right kind of fuel in your system if you want it to operate efficiently. The body has to use too much energy to process and digest substances that are not good for it—energy you need for the other areas of your life, energy you deserve to have available to you. When your body is functioning at its optimum, as a result of healthy eating and regular exercise, you will be amazed by how good you feel. Experiment with a few changes for a week or two just to see the difference.

Incorporating daily meditation, rigorous exercise, and healthy eating into your life takes time. Do it one day at a time and you will be pleased with the long-term results. Initially, making change creates stress. As both short and long-term benefits appear you will feel encouraged by the positive choices you are making—choices to know your body and your inner world more intimately, choices to take care of yourself.

Beyond these basic and major changes there are additional helpful, healthy steps to take for growth and change and release from powerlessness. Some have been mentioned throughout the book so explore them with the idea of using what fits for you right now.

(1) Take your emotional, physical temperature several times a day.

(2) Use affirmations verbally and/or in writing.

(3) Write in a journal regularly.

(4) Read and/or attend workshops for your growth and development.

(5) Attend regular 12-step meetings if you are codependent, an adult child of an alcoholic, in recovery from an addiction or if you are beginning to confront and identify addictive behavior.

(6) Consider individual and/or group therapy if you are not functioning well on your own.

Taking Your Temperature

Taking your emotional and physical temperature several times a day is a method of checking in with yourself. Consider how many times a day you unconsciously check yourself in a mirror or catch your reflection in a shop window. Check yourself out with conscious awareness. Take two or three deep breaths. Have you been breathing deeply or holding your breath or breathing in a shallow manner? How does your body feel? Are you moving or working too rapidly? What emotions are you aware of? What thoughts are in the foreground of your mind? You can review all these things in just a few minutes. In doing so, you are increasing your awareness of yourself. If things feel hectic, difficult or negative, stay with those feelings. Then, recognize this awareness as an opportunity to identify what you are needing. Slow down and rethink whatever you are doing. Redirect yourself to behavior that results in positive feelings.

Affirmations

Begin to use affirmations on a regular basis. Once it becomes a habit, the verbal part is easy. For example, begin your morning by talking to yourself in the bathroom mirror. Use the all-purpose affirmation, "I, (your name), am calm, relaxed, and alert, ready to handle the day effectively." Such behavior may initially make you feel a little awkward. Gradually, if you practice regularly, you will warm to the process. You will find yourself smiling at your reflection and feeling the energy positive regard gives you.

The best affirmations are those constructed in your own words and based on the specific things on which you are working. The verbal ones are easy to carry with you everywhere. To write affirmations takes a little more time. Write the affirmation you have constructed on the left hand side of a piece of paper, perhaps in your journal. Listen for the disclaimer and write it down, precisely as you hear it, on the other side of the page. Write the affirmation again. Listen for and write the disclaimer. The disclaimer may be the same or it may be a new one. Continue to write the affirmation until you become aware that the disclaimers are silent. It helps to write affirmations at the end of a meditation, but you may choose to work with these concepts any time. If you have just come from a difficult meeting, sit quietly and write some affirming statements to center yourself. Prepare for a difficult meeting in the same manner. Once you become familiar with such a process, you can calm and center yourself in two or three minutes.

Keeping a Journal

Keeping a journal is a way to the inner self that has been used for thousands of years. Writing about your physical awareness, thoughts, feelings, behaviors, and spiritual life is a way of opening and maintaining communication with the unconscious. To begin, find a notebook that appeals to you, preferably loose leaf, and choose a time during the day when you will have some time to yourself to reflect in writing. For many, this is first thing in the morning. For others, it is the last thing before going to bed. Still others use their lunch hour at work!

There are many formats and structures for beginning a journal. Write at least one sentence (and as much more as you want) about the following:

(1) My body: What am I aware of physically? Do I feel good? Am I in any pain? Are there any symptoms I need to pay attention to?

(2) My thoughts: What is in the foreground? What is bothering me today? What am I excited about, focused on? What have I learned?

(3) My feelings: What words accurately describe my feeling state? Happy, sad, anxious, depressed, or joyful? How have I felt throughout this day?

(4) My spiritual life: Am I in contact with my higher self? My higher power? Is there a sense of fullness or of loving? Do I feel distant from myself and others?

As you write, try not to censor or edit. The writing is for you and there is no need to try to make it look or sound perfect. Efforts at perfection will defeat your purpose. If you write in a steam of consciousness with no attention to spelling, punctuation, or detail, your writing will eventually flow out of you rather than being forced. When the flow begins, you will sometimes find you are writing things that surprise you: "I had no idea I was feeling _____." "If that is what I have been thinking and telling myself, no wonder I have been so low." Through this process you gain insight.

Reading/Attending Workshops

Reading and/or attending workshops will keep you alive and thinking and feeling. Gradually a great deal of the work we do on ourselves becomes exciting and fulfilling rather than threatening and painful. Sometimes it is helpful to label the nature of our work. Remediation is a good word to define some of our early work on ourselves. It is repair; it is healing old wounds; it is developing the undeveloped or underdeveloped areas of the self. Remediation is the hard part. Then comes maintenance, growth and self-actualization which are increasingly easier. There is no pain-free life, no easy ride, but you get better at knowing how to breathe deeply and work through the painful and stuck spots. Consequently, continued reading and learning is an all-important part of your process. There is a book available or a workshop being offered on every subject mentioned thus far, so your priority-setting skills become important. Your goal-setting becomes essential.

Attending 12-Step Meetings

In 1935, Alcoholics Anonymous was established and 12-step meetings came into being. The significance and success of these leaderless, non-hierarchical support groups is evident merely in their proliferation. Twelve-step meetings can be found in nearly every community. There are meetings for alcoholics, drug-users, overeaters, gamblers, sexual addicts, workaholics, adult children of alcoholics, and codependents. The model works so well that additional 12-step meetings are probably being formed as you read. As you explore and look for the best meeting for you, make certain the group uses the 12-step format. Sometimes in newly formed adult children and codependent groups, the steps are not utilized. The steps are essential to recovery. Depending on your need, these groups are available for support, for teaching a process of coping, and establishing a spiritual pathway. They are free of charge. Support helps, and attending a 12-step meeting related to your area of recovery is a good starting point. Give it a try once or twice and then evaluate your experience.

Individual and/or Group Therapy

It is important not to wait or wonder if you have reached a point of needing professional help. Make a phone call and ask for a consultation if you are in doubt. Ask a friend about the therapist s/he sees and how the decision was made to seek out a therapist. Friends or colleagues can sometimes shortcut the process of deciding where to get therapy by recommending two or three psychologists or social workers.

If you decide to begin therapy, your choice of a therapist is important. Be in charge of the decision by gathering information through any references you have obtained and through interviewing the therapists you call. Make certain the individual you are questioning is familiar with the psychology of women. Make sure the therapist has experience with women who live the life you live; whether you are a career woman, a radical feminist, a traditional mother, or a lesbian. Be direct. Ask questions about the individual's credentials and training. Have they read any of the books you think are important (or any you see in the references here)? Do they know anything about codependence or addictions? Do they offer groups? Are they familiar with 12-step programs? Remember, when you encounter a therapist who is defensive about being interviewed, you are talking to the wrong person.

If you have identified addictive behavior in your relationships and/or life-style, if you see that you are codependent and that powerlessness has been a major theme in your life, you will eventually find group therapy very helpful. If it sounds terrible and frightening at first (and it does to many of us), start with individual work. Groups are an essential part of effectively moving through the kinds of problems we have been discussing. Often a combination of group and individual work is powerful.

Whatever your decision, it is permissible to ask for help. One hallmark of being stuck is the belief that "I should be able to figure this out on my own." "I don't want anyone to know what's going on with me." Tell someone how you feel. Begin talking out loud rather than to yourself, and gradually you will be able to determine the best direction for yourself.

Change Starts With You

As you review and reflect on what steps you will take next in your recovery, remember that the only person you can change is you. This is a hard reality to learn and digest. Once you "get it," you are truly on your way. Once you accept it, you know where to begin. Even when you know with certainty that life would be fine if your spouse, significant other, kid, mother or boss would behave differently, remember you have no control over the behaviors, thoughts, and feelings of others. You can, however, be *in charge* of you. No matter how perfectly right you are, you can find something to change in your behavior, your attitude, or your perception of what is happening. Begin to do it and you will experience taking back your personal power.

What happens when you alter your own behavior? When you choose to change your behavior, your way of responding in a relationship or in a specific conversation or situation, you make a powerful change in you. When you change you create a *potential* for change in the individual with whom you are interacting.

Remember, you can not actually change the other person, just yourself. However, when you change your behavior/response, there is a shift in the relationship and in the balance of power in the relationship. The old familiar way of interacting has been shaken. The person you are talking to will feel the shift and then s/he must decide how to respond.

Established patterns of interactions are like scripts for a play. Imagine you and the person you are talking to are each reading from scripts. You rely on one another to stick to the script so that you each know what to say next. Expectations develop, a pattern evolves. Then you decide to ad lib. You alter your lines. You change your behavior. You move away from the expectation of reading the script as it is written. What happens? The other person may be temporarily thrown off guard, become uncomfortable, confused or even embarrassed or angry. S/he may repeat her/his last line, giving you the opportunity to "get it right." You persist in your individual change. What must the other do? S/he may choose to:

(1) Persist in trying to get you to read the script the way it should be read/do what "you always do."
(2) Become angry or punishing.
(3) Leave the conversation altogether.
(4) Listen to what you have been saying and *change* to stay in compatible conversation with you.

Generally, when you change, you can initially count on the other person to stage a countermove, to do something to get you to behave the way you usually behave. Persistence on your part is critical at this stage. As you maintain your position and continue the change you have initiated, the other person must eventually alter what s/he is doing. You may not like the change at first, but change will take place.

Here's another visual image. On the tennis court, you often lose when you are receiving the serve, when the other person is hitting balls into your end of the court. Typical tennis behavior (as well as typical conversational behavior) is to hit the ball back. This means you are playing the game. It usually means the other person is in charge. Instead, imagine that you step out of the way and let the ball bounce out of your end of the court. *You don't have to respond.* Many additional balls may come at you so you have to be quick on your feet and sharp witted. The expectation is that the individual will eventually run out of balls. Then you can serve your own. Now you are in charge.

The process of change is complex. That is why it is so essential to begin with yourself. You have been given a great deal to think about, to digest, to consider in your own process. Take your time, establish your own pace, create your own pathway for the journey, but begin. Your authentic self, struggling to be released from powerlessness, depends on taking that first step.

Exploring, Questioning, Reflecting

Ask yourself where you can honestly begin the process of letting go and taking charge of releasing negative patterns of behavior. What can you realistically expect of yourself based on what life is like right now? What are you already doing that deserves validation? Are there ways you typically "rein in" your success or keep yourself from being as powerful as you can be? (Like expecting too much; not being honest with yourself; minimizing or rationalizing your behavior?)

1. Make a list of ways you might "rein in" or slow your own growth.

2. Identify ways to get help/or help yourself with each thing you have listed.

3. List your expectations of yourself. Are they realistic?

4. Set goals that feel realistic for you.

5. Refer to the resources at the end of the book for more ideas.

CHAPTER 9

FOR (AND ABOUT) MEN

"I would probably lose my husband and my job if I let all my personal power out. I would have to find another environment to live and work in."

"Be a more successful supervisor. Divorce my husband. Meet more people and develop many friendships."

"My husband would cheer. I would feel relief and exhilarated."

I have learned one all purpose important fact about men. When a woman questions, "What are you feeling? What's wrong?" He is not lying when he replies, "I don't know."

This basic "exchange"—definitely not communication—has taken place in my office many times with many couples. The woman asks the question, receives the reply, and becomes either sad, agitated, or angry. The man looks scared and depressed and stares at the floor or out the window, avoiding eye contact. They have both been in this interaction before. My usual intervention is to say to him, "I know you are telling the truth." Or, to her, "He really is telling the truth."

The underlying truth in this example is that the man *is feeling* a feeling. He, however, usually has no language to name what it is. He often has very little experience with feeling, identifying or naming what is going on, and expressing it openly to the person who wants to know. The task is for men to learn words to describe emotions, then to experience a "felt sense"* that the word fits the emotional and/or physical sensation he is having. The process of a man learning to make the association between feelings and identifying a word to describe the feeling is sometimes long and hard. But, it is rewarding. I have seen men struggle and have seen the relief on their faces and in their bodies when they are able to make the connection between their heads and their hearts. I have also seen the relief on the faces of the women who are spouses or significant others. Communication can at last begin.

Men and Power

What is the relationship between this concept of feeling, or expressing feelings, and power? For men in our culture, the belief is that power means *not feeling.* Power is thinking and acting, usually in the absence of any outward indication of feeling. Certainly, in reality, feelings are present. For some, feelings are right below the surface, creating identifiable conflict; for others, feelings are buried more deeply.

Our cultural beliefs also suggest feelings are reserved for women and thinking is reserved for men. Power is associated with thinking. How logical then that it is assumed men have power and women don't! White men have most of the power in our culture, and in general they have only one kind, positional power. They have positions of power in our institutions and organizations. Because so many men abuse positional power, the majority of our organizations/institutions are stressful, workaholic, unhealthy places.

Personal power, the ability to create one's own environment, is usually missing for men. Men may outwardly appear to have

---

*See *Focusing* by Eugene Gendlin for more information on this concept.

more of it than women, but generally they are demonstrating "pseudo personal power." True personal power comes from a connection with the authentic self, from a connection with the heart as well as the head. In the absence of either, personal power is diminished or artificial.

Men learn to hide their authentic selves at an early age just as women do. But the process for men is different because we emphasize such opposite tasks/learnings/directions for little boys and girls. We teach boys to "color outside the lines." We teach them to place their primary focus on tasks or work. We teach them to think and to deny what they feel and we validate aggression and competitive behavior. While men do cooperate, collaborate, and communicate, the purpose of the behavior is usually to complete a task, to win a game or to produce a widget rather than to nurture or develop a relationship.

Power in the male model—the dominant model of our society—is associated with thinking, competing, winning, and particularly with making money. Power in the male model is physical; it has no heart and no compassion. Power, in reality, is a neutral energy force—one which can be used positively or negatively. In our culture, while we have moved in the direction of warping and abusing power, more and more men and women are beginning to recognize the overall negative effects of such abuse on the self, the family, the organization, the world and the universe.

Just as women are assumed to be power*less*, men are assumed to be power*ful*. The expectations for men include being right, being knowledgeable, being courageous and taking risks. They are not supposed to feel fear or grief or pain. One acceptable feeling for men is anger. Consequently, anger is frequently the feeling expressed even if the real, underlying emotion is fear, grief, or pain. The expectations on men are oppressive to the self. The denial of the genuine feeling or the authentic self creates many of the same kinds of physical, behavioral, emotional, and spiritual stress described for women in chapter 2. A major difference for men is more physical symptoms. More men than women have heart attacks, high blood pressure, and strokes. The life span of men is 7 to 10 years shorter than that of women.

Stress in men seems to manifest more frequently in serious physical problems because there is so little permission to identify or feel the behavioral, emotional and spiritual symptoms.

Men's Roles

As you reflect on what you've learned about powerlessness, codependence, and addictions, it's easy to see that men, too, are powerless and codependent. They are, consequently, at high risk for addictions. Men, like women, need to retrieve the authentic self. It is often much more difficult because the process of identifying and feeling feelings conflicts with society's expectations of men. The definition of a real man, a desirable man, a successful man doesn't, historically, include feeling and displaying feelings.

In other words, men's lives are defined by boxes too. While the box defining men allows the development of positional power and more intellectual, physical, political, professional, personal freedom, it is limiting to the real or authentic self. Visualize the boxes for men and women. The box that defines women's roles and expectations is small, stationary and confining. The box that defines roles and expectations for men is much larger, less confining, and mobile—it's on wheels!

Test a different kind of freedom or flexibility. Women have been "trying on" some of the behaviors of men in our society. We are developing our "male energy." That means we have been struggling to move out into the world of work, develop our capacities to think, solve problems, make decisions, and experience success and fulfillment in places other than the home. Metaphorically, we have been moving cautiously out of our box and engaging in life experiences and behaviors traditionally labeled "for men only." As mobile and powerful as men are, what happens when they "try on" the behaviors of women in our society? When they move to develop "female energy"?

Frequently, men who are sensitive, nurturing, vulnerable, compassionate, intuitive; men who decide to become primary caregivers to children while their wives or significant others work outside the home or participate in tasks such as cooking and maintaining the household, are rejected by other men—and sometimes by women. There is little permission for men to test out our traditional roles and expectations. I remember, for example, making life miserable for the brother of a childhood friend. He hated athletics and other "traditional" male activities and loved to cook. Not only did we make fun of him, we used him, by making him fix breakfast on overnights or threatening him if he didn't bake brownies for us! (Somehow he has developed into an adult who still enjoys cooking!)

Unfortunately there are serious and disturbing reasons for the barrier against allowing men to develop their "female" energy and interests. The primary reason is that what women *do* is undervalued in the culture and, therefore, seen as powerless. So why would a man want to learn such powerless behaviors or roles? Why would men want to learn to feel, to parent, to value relationships over tasks? The imbalance of power in our society, and the powerlessness of women limits the development of the authentic self of both women and men. It limits us from knowing who we really are, liking it, owning it, and taking back our personal power.

Relationships

How does this imbalance, these limitations, affect men's relationships with women and with other men? Some details about our backgrounds helps answer these questions. Remember that boys and girls are socialized in parallel but significantly different directions. Boys are taught to focus on tasks and work and girls are taught to focus on relationships. The socialization is intended to be complimentary! Boys will grow up and become men who think for, work for, and protect women; girls will grow up and become women who feel for, nurture for, parent for, and create a home for men. This type of socialization is limiting to individual development and it creates a different world view for each sex. We end up with two adults of the opposite sex living together and working together, yet their way of viewing the world or perceiving reality is dramatically different. To say, then, that women and men have trouble communicating, either at home or at work, is one of the largest understatements we can make. How then do we build good loving or working relationships?

We begin by understanding the real problem. It is not a communication problem. It is a difference in values. Sometimes talking with a member of the opposite sex feels like being parachuted into a foreign country where we don't speak the language. We feel afraid, uncertain, and insecure. On a much deeper level than we can recognize in day-to-day conversation, many men are afraid of women. Also, many women are afraid of men. Both men and women carry old wounds from childhood. Unresolved pain, fear and anger with the opposite sex parent is often carried forward into our personal and work relationships. Old feelings contaminate current relationships and add to the fear we sometimes have for the opposite sex.

To continue to learn about being male and female, we are pushed to identify with the same sex parent in our families. Because little boys are supposed to be like Daddy, very early in the developmental process the little boy is pushed away from Mother; pushed in the direction of Father or of male role models. In most families this process of separation takes place too early. The little boy is not ready to break the bond with the primary parent who in our society is usually the mother. The trauma of being pushed "out of the nest" before the normal dependency needs have been fulfilled can be traumatic. If father is absent emotionally and physically, he is not able to support and model for the male child. In dysfunctional or addictive families the little boy loses his childhood. He grows up too fast and becomes the "little man" of the family, taking on too early, the role of protector. These processes contribute to the formation of strong barriers against intimacy. The need to protect the self is a dominant feeling that develops early.

For girls the bond with the primary parent, usually the mother, is maintained because this is also the source for the same sex identity formation. And in most families the separation process comes too late. Mother and daughter stay connected (sometimes enmeshed) and learning about appropriate boundaries in relationships is delayed. Just as with boys, girls in dysfunctional or addictive families must grow up too fast. They do not get to be little, to have their dependency needs met. They either share with mother or take over the caretaker role and become the "little woman."

The result of the dysfunction in the developmental process is adults who did not get to be children long enough. When we have not been fully dependent we have trouble being truly autonomous. When we have trouble being autonomous, we have trouble being intimate. We have men who set boundaries that are too strong or too rigid; men who protect themselves from intimacy. We have women who do too little to set boundaries and desire intimacy to the extent of allowing people to inappropriately cross the boundary of the self. We have, in short, individuals who are ill-equipped for true intimacy; either with members of the opposite or same sex.

How do men relate to one another? Observations from male clients and reports from male friends suggest some men want and are struggling to form relationships with each other that include true intimacy. It is hard. How can you be open, honest, and intimate with someone when you are supposed to be more powerful than he is? How can you expose a genuine feeling when, in the male world, such exposure threatens your image as a real or successful man, a man who is in control and one who has power because he does not show his feelings?

Years ago a man started therapy with me because his wife had left him. He was extremely depressed and as we explored the problem, I checked to see what kind of support he had in his life without his wife. Who did he talk to, spend time with? I was relieved to learn he had a consistent group of male friends. Weekly they played basketball together and had dinner afterwards. This was a long-standing group of almost five years. When I asked if he was getting enough support from these friends, he looked puzzled and confused. Even as I was asking the question, I realized why. He had never told these friends his wife had left him!

In a flash I visualized women in the same situation. The female group would have known about the problem before they got together for their weekly activity because they would have had regular contact—either by phone or in person. Some of them would have already cried with the woman who was separated or shared anger, even rage with her about what a jerk her husband was to leave. The woman would have received emotional support because women form relationships for the sake of relating. Men, on the other hand, appear more likely to get together around an activity. They seem to *do* things together rather than *be* together.

Occasionally I have suggested to male clients that they ask a male friend to have lunch or dinner with them. Dozens of these male clients have again looked puzzled or asked why. They believe they would need a reason for doing so, a specific agenda, a work related question to pose, or a meal that would precede or follow an activity such as a sports event. When I suggest the possibility of just talking, most men feel uneasy or embarrassed. They worry about what the other man might think. Some exhibit homophobia. Very few men have cultural or internal permission to explore intimate friendships with one another and so as a result men lose a great deal of the intimacy and support they deserve. They lose the opportunity to examine and discuss with one another who they are or who they are becoming. More opportunities are lost for the expression of the authentic self and personal power continues to diminish.

Most men have a great deal of work to do on themselves to regain true personal power, to experience recovery from codependence, and to identify any addictions. They can benefit from any of the exercises, activities, or reading suggestions in this book.

Exploring, Questioning, Reflecting

1. What is really important to me in my life today? If I knew this was my last day on earth, how and with whom would I spend it?

2. How do I feel at this moment; physically, emotionally, and spiritually? Remember that "I don't know" is an acceptable answer, but push yourself a little and look at the lists below to see if any of these words fit.

FEELING WORD CHECK LIST FOR MEN

FEAR

apprehensive	frightened	mistrustful	inadequate
terror	panic	afraid	scared
leary	spooked	horror	awe
uneasy	fearful	reverence	paranoid
anxiety	skeptical	doubtful	alarmed

ANGER

rage	uptight	mad	pissed
furious	inflamed	infuriated	fury
angry	annoyed	irritated	resentment
enraged	provoked	accosted	irate
hot	upset	indignant	wrath
hostile	animosity		

SAD

bummed	uncertain	cheerless	disappointed
depressed	failure	gloomy	unhappy
sorrow	sorrowful	dismay	regret
downcast	dejected	mournful	blue
low	brooding	shameful	somber
discontented	worried	timid	helpless
woeful	melancholy		

HELPLESS

powerless	defenseless	crippled
dependent	destitute	resourceless
lost	impotent	spent
exhausted	defeated	abandoned
feeble	weak	inefficient
vulnerable	incompetent	depleted

HATE

vengeance	hateful	detest
bitter	spite	
hostile	resentment	loathing
disfavor		

dislike	animosity	despise
adverse	bitterness	disaffection
abhorance	envy	

OPPRESSED

down	afflicted	tyrannized
overtaken	burdened	used
captive	crushed	crossed
misused	persecuted	mistreated
trampled	overpowered	subdued
captive	pushed	pressured
trodden		

DISAPPOINTED

failure	failed	hurt
unfulfilled	downcast	unsuccessful
discontent	unhappy	unsatisfied
disillusioned	let-down	discouraged
disenchanted		

JOY

happy	elation	pleasure
gaiety	spirited	turned-on
freaked-out	wired-up	elated
mellow	beautiful	contentment
exuberant	glad	triumphant
jubilant	mirth	wonderful
terrific	jazzed	delighted

LOVE

loving	caring	admiration
passion	befriended	affectionate
desiring	infatuation	adoring
concern	regard	empathy
appreciation	completeness	togetherness
rejoiceful	adulation	

EPILOGUE

SOME FINAL THOUGHTS

My work facilitates connections with hundreds of amazing women all over the country, and I am grateful for the individuals I meet and the things I learn from the encounters. So many bright women ask hard questions, and I am continually stretched in my thinking about women and power.

Regardless of the level of accomplishment women attain, relationships appear to remain as the core concern of the majority, whether at home or at work. Consequently, I continue to think about what's important if we are to honor who we are and allow that focus to be such a central part of our lives. What can we do or attend to, to be more effective, fulfilled, powerful? If you can only focus on a few things, I recommend these basic thoughts.

Pay Attention, Particularly to Your Need for Control

Women (and men, too) are so often focused on their own interior process that it is easy to miss, or misinterpret, what's right in front of you. The level of stress most individuals experience today is close to disabling! It is thus essential to slow down and look around you each day. Notice the people, the events, the bigger picture, and particularly, notice your own projections. What is really happening around you rather than what you assume, interpret, guess at, even make up in your own mind? If you're moving too fast, you miss much of your day by being on automatic pilot.

Take a deep breath and see what happens when you release your need to be in control, to be right, to be perfect, to have things turn out the way you want, to have people think and feel and do it the way you do. When you can let go of being in control, you are paying attention, and you have increased the probability that you can instead be "in charge of your own environment" and have the impact you are striving for.

Listen Like You've Never Listened Before

Because you invest so much time and energy in relationships, you may easily convince yourself that you're a good listener. Try this test. If you can't paraphrase everything the other person is saying to you, then you're not really listening. If you're absolutely certain you're right about whatever is being discussed, you *can't* be listening. You can improve the quality of every relationship you are in by first, listening to the person with whom you're talking, and then listening just as carefully to yourself. This level of attentiveness moves you to dialogue, negotiation, ease in interacting, and obviously, dramatically improved communication and connection.

Be a Role Model or a Mentor—or Both

All over the country the most common question I'm asked is how can I teach my daughter to be powerful? By *showing* her what it looks like. When you take care of yourself, exercise power, lead a healthy life, you multiply the likelihood that any young woman in your immediate environment will be impacted positively. Most young women could use a mentor, so perhaps you can do that, too.

Avoid Collusion. Your Mind Is "Infected" By the Culture You've Grown Up In.

Changing behavior is extraordinarily difficult when everything you have learned, growing up female, teaches you to believe and behave in many ways that aren't good for you. The thinking is ingrained. The behavior is automatic. Watch for the ways you collude in the process of negating yourself and other women. Without self-examination, you are likely to think about yourself and other women the same way your parents, teachers, and young female and male peers did. Do some healthy housecleaning of your belief system about yourself as a woman/about other women/about men.

Quit Being Nice—Please!

Trade being nice for being good, loving, caring, and supportive. But please stop being nice. It is self-negating. When you are nice, it's generally because you are fearful, anxious, or guilt ridden. You want to be a people pleaser. You want others to think you are a good _____(fill in the blank). When your focus is to please others because you fear they won't like you, love you, or approve of your behavior, you give your power away. You disappear.

Figure Out Self-Care . . . Finally . . . And Do It

Put yourself first. If you take care of yourself, you actually multiply your energy for doing good and loving things for those you care about. The bonus in this process is lack of resentment, a return of energy, and a smile on your face. When your needs have been at least partially met, you can enjoy giving of yourself to others. When you come last on your own list, you may find yourself gritting your teeth as you volunteer time and energy for all those who need something from you. You don't like what you're doing and feel even worse about yourself because you *believe* you should give lovingly. Figure out what is most important to you. Ask for what you want. Learn to say no when you need to do so. Saying no can change your life—positively.

Be Powerful

Above all, be powerful. When you choose to give power away you become either a victim or a persecutor. Those are the only choices. In a powerless state, you feel everyone is against you and nothing ever goes your way, or you are filled with negative thoughts about successful people and calculating your next revenge on someone you resent. These are seriously stuck states of being that slip away when you move into healthy uses of power. Go for it!

Recommendations for Reading

The Lens of Gender — Sandra Bem
Life Is a Miracle — Wendell Berry
All That Is Solid Melts Into Air — Marshall Berman
Where to Go From Here — James E. Birren and Linda Feldman
On Dialogue — David Bohm
The Answer to How Is Yes — Peter Block
Stewardship — Peter Block
Women's Inhumanity to Women — Phyllis Chessler
The Tao of Negotiation — Joel Edelman and Mary Beth Crain
Circle of Stones: Woman's Journey to Herself — Judith Duerk
The Power of Partnership — Riane Eisler
The First Sex — Helen Fisher
The Tipping Point — Malcolm Galdwell
The Birth of Pleasure — Carol Gilligan
Real Power — Janet Hagberg
The Tao of Leadership — John Heider
Dialogue and the Art of Thinking Together — William Isaacs
Leadership: The Inner Side of Greatness — Peter Koestenbaum
The Dance of Connection — Harriet Lerner
The Careless Society — John McKnight
In the Absence of the Sacred — Jerry Mander
The Heroine's Journey — Maureen Murdock
Let Your Life Speak — Parker Palmer
Speaking of Sex: The Denial of Gender Inequality — Deborah L. Rhode
Facing the World With Soul — Robert Sardello
The Confident Woman — Marjorie Shaevitz
How Can I Get Through to You — Terrance Real
Why So Slow — Virgnia Valian
Addiction to Perfection — Marion Woodman
Crucial Conventions — Kerry Patterson, Joseph Grenny, Ron McMillan and Al Switzler

Appendices

Appendix A

Readings—Ideas—Resources

The information provided in this section is divided into the nine steps to release identified in Chapter 8.

1. Daily Meditation or Relaxation Exercises

Readings

- *Focusing*—Eugene Gendlin
- *Creative Visualization*—Shakti Gawain
- *A Gradual Awakening*—Stephen Levine
- *The Art of Breathing*—Nancy Zi
- *Freedom in Meditation*—Patricia Carrington

Ideas and Resources

- Try practicing the technique at the end of Chapter 2 for a few weeks. Then move on to a more advanced technique.
- Consider attending a class on meditation or relaxation techniques. Often, such classes are free or offered inexpensively through women's centers or "free/alternative universities."
- Often your local health food store can be an unexpected resource. Stop by and see if they have information.
- Get a massage to loosen up physical barriers to relaxation. Get a direct referral from a friend or colleague.
- Experiment with audio relaxation tapes. I suggest those done by Dr. Emmett Miller. They are available through Source In California—1-800-52TAPES.

2. Regular and rigorous exercise

Readings

- *The Aerobics Program for Total Well-Being*—Kenneth Cooper
- *Quantum Fitness*—Irving Dardik and Dennis Waitley

Ideas and Resources

- Visualize yourself exercising. Spend 5 minutes of your morning seeing yourself playfully and gracefully doing the activity of your choice. See yourself smiling, happy and energetic. Do this for seven days before beginning your activity.
- Make a list of all the pros and cons of beginning an exercise program.
- Ask your inner child what kind of exercise s/he would prefer.
- Call the physical education or athletic department of a local college or school for information on exercise facilities/programs.
- Explore any fitness centers available.
- Obtain a physical examination before beginning an exercise program.

3. A Healthy Eating Plan

Readings

- *Jane Brody's Nutrition Book*—Jane Brody
- *Good Food Book*—Jane Brody
- *The New American Diet*—Sonja L. Connor and William E. Connor
- *The Only Diet There Is*—Sandra Ray

Ideas and Resources

- Form a support group to assist you in your transition.
- If you discover a real addiction to food, join Overeaters Anonymous. It is listed in the phone book. You might also call the National Council on Alcoholism or your local mental health association.

4. Take Your Emotional, Physical Temperature

Readings

Use the same books suggested for meditation and relaxation

Ideas/Resources

- Check in with yourself three times a day. First thing in the morning (while washing your face, brushing your teeth); sometime around lunch; and at bedtime. Just smile at yourself in the mirror—and check in—ask yourself how you're doing. Say an affirmation out loud. It might sound a little silly and feel self-conscious, but you will begin to enjoy it.

5. Affirm Yourself

Readings

- *I Deserve Love*—Sandra Ray

Ideas and Resources

- Form a group of 4 or 5 friends. Meet regularly to read the book, learn to write affirmations, practice together.
- Practice affirmations daily.

6. Journal Regularly

Readings

- *At a Journal Workshop*—Ira Prokoff
- *Inner Work*—Robert Johnson,

Ideas and Resources

- Attend a journal workshop if you want more specific techniques.
- Call your local mental health association or mental health agency, or private practioners for information.
- Write regularly.

7. Read and/or Attend Workshops for Your Growth and Development

General Reading

The Assertive Woman—Nancy Austin and Stanlee Phelps
In Transition—Judith Bardwick
Women's Ways of Knowing—Belenky, Clinchy, Golberger, Tarule
The Empowered Manager—Peter Block
The New Partnership: Women and Men in Organizations—Nina L. Colwill
Diving Deep and Surfacing—Carol Crist
The Male Machine—Marc Fasteau
In a Different Voice—Carol Gilligan
When and Where I Enter: Impact of Black Women on Race and Sex in America— Paula Giddings
The Hazards of Being Male—Herb Goldberg
Powers of the Weak—Elizabeth Janeway
Is This Where I Was Going—Natasha Josefowitz
Paths to Power—Natasha Josefowitz
Who Is the Boss—Natasha Josefowitz
Men and Women of the Corporation—Rosabeth Kanter
An Unknown Woman—Alice Kohler
The Wounded Woman—Linda Leonard
The Dance of Anger—Harriet G. Lerner
The Dance of Intimacy—Harriet G. Lerner
Women in Therapy—Harriet G. Lerner
Breakthrough: Women into Management—Loring and Wells
Energy and Personal Power—Shirley Luthman
Power—The Inner Experience—David McClelland
Toward a New Psychology of Women—Jean Baker Miller
Between Women—Susie Orbach and Luise Eichenbaum
Understanding Women—Susie Orbach and Luise Eichenbaum
What Do Women Want—Susie Orbach and Luise Eichenbaum
The Myth of Masculinity—Joseph Pleck

At a Journal Workshop–Ira Progoff
You're In Charge–Becoming Your Own Therapist–
    Jeannette Rainwater
On Personal Power–Carl Rogers
The Androgynous Manager– Alice Sargent
Beyond Sex Roles–Alice Sargent (2nd Edition) See
    "Issues for Women in Organizations" by Linda L.
    Moore.
Escape From Intimacy–Anne Wilson Schaef
Women's Realities–Anne Wilson Schaef
The Superwoman Syndrome–Marjorie Shaevitz
About Time–Kay Cronkite Waldo and Alex Mackenzie
Winning by Negotiation–Tesa Albert Warschau
Networking–Mary Scott Welch

Readings on Addiction and Codependence

*Alcoholism and Women: The Background and the
    Psychology*–Jan Bauer
Repeat After Me (workbook for Adult Children of
Alcoholics)–Claudia Black
Out of the Shadow–Patrick Carnes
Diagnosing and Treating Co-Dependence–
    Timmen L. Cermak
The Observing Self–Arthur J. Deikman
Fat is a Family Affair–Judi Hollis
Shame–The Power of Caring–Gershen Kaufman
The Psychodynamics of Alcoholism: A Current Synthesis–
    William J. Haugen Light (See the entire series of
    five books.)
Facing Codependence–Pia Melody
After the Tears–Jane Middleton-Moz and Lorie Dwinell
Your Inner Child of the Past–Hugh Missildine
Women Who Love Too Much–Robin Norwood
Playing Ball on Running Water–David K. Reynolds
The Addicted Organization–Anne Wilson Schaef and
    Diane Passel
Codependence–Misunderstood, Mistreated–Anne Wilson
    Schaef

When Society Becomes an Addict—Anne Wilson Schaef
The Transformers—Jacqueline Small
The Natural History of Alcoholism—George Vaillant
Choicemaking—Sharon Wegscheider-Cruse
*Another Chance: Hope and Health for the Alcoholic
     Family*—Sharon Wegscheider-Cruse
Alcoholism and Spirituality—Charles Whitfield
Healing the Child Within—Charles Whitfield
Addiction to Perfection—Marion Woodman
Struggle for Intimacy—Janet Geringer Woititz

8. Attend 12-Step Meetings

Readings

- *The 12-Steps for Adult Children*—Recovery Publications
- *The 12-Steps-A Way Out—A Working Guide for Adult
  Children of Alcoholics and Other Dysfunctional
  Families*—Recovery Publications

Ideas and Resources

- Call the National Council on Alcoholism and Drug
  Dependence. In Kansas City the number is
  816-361-5900.
- Attend an open Alcoholics Anonymous meeting. The
  National Council will tell you about them.
- Ask for separate numbers for contacts for: ALANON,
  Adult Children of Alcoholics, Overeaters Anonymous,
  Sex Anonymous, Codependents Anonymous, Gamblers
  Anonymous, Narcotics Anonymous. These may be
  listed in the phone book.
- Attend a meeting and ask people for information on
  additional meetings.
- Call any mental health agency or association for
  information.

9. Consider Individual and/or Group Therapy.

Readings

You're In Charge—Becoming Your Own Therapist— Jeanette Rainwater

*The Superwoman Syndrome—*Marjorie Shaevitz

*Women's Realities—*Anne Wilson Schaef

*The Dance of Anger—*Harriet G. Lerner

*Women in Therapy—*Harriet G. Lerner

*Playing Ball on Running Water—*David Reynolds

*Assertive Woman—*Stanlee Phelps and Nancy Austin

*I Deserve Love—*Sondra Ray

*Understanding Women—*Susie Orbach and Luise Eichenbaum

*What Do Women Want—*Susie Orbach and Luise Eichenbaum

*The Drama of the Gifted Child—*Alice Miller

Ideas and Resources

- Call the National Council for therapists who have experience and/or specialize in working with codependence and addictions.
- Get direct referrals from friends, family members, professionals, mental health associations.
- Ask for names of several therapists.
- Interview therapists before deciding on who you will hire.

APPENDIX B

Appendix B contains charts from references. These charts are: The Development of Codependence, The Development of Addictions, and An Illustration of the Location of the Seven Chakras.

The Development of Codependence

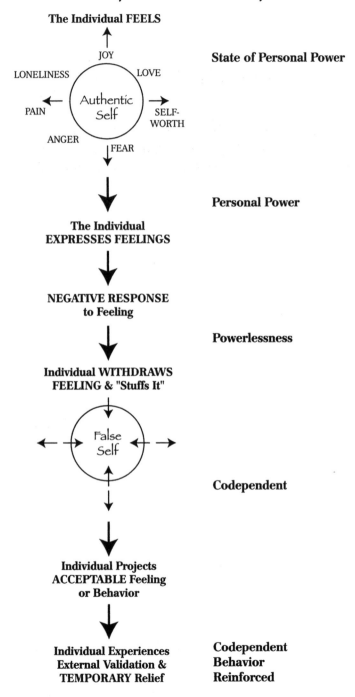

The Individual FEELS

JOY

LONELINESS   LOVE

Authentic Self

PAIN   SELF-WORTH

ANGER   FEAR

State of Personal Power

The Individual EXPRESSES FEELINGS

Personal Power

NEGATIVE RESPONSE to Feeling

Powerlessness

Individual WITHDRAWS FEELING & "Stuffs It"

False Self

Codependent

Individual Projects ACCEPTABLE Feeling or Behavior

Individual Experiences External Validation & TEMPORARY Relief

Codependent Behavior Reinforced

The Development of Addictions

**Individual Finds Ways
TO MEDICATE
Unacceptable Feelings**

↓

**Individual Experiences
RELIEF**

↓

**Individual REPEATS PATTERN
and Assoicates Relief with
Medicating Substance or Process**

**Ritual Behavior/Compulsions/
Obsessions**

↓

**ADDICTION DEVELOPS
and Feelings Grow
Stronger and Move
Deeper "Underground"**

Powerlessness

The Locations of the Seven Chakras

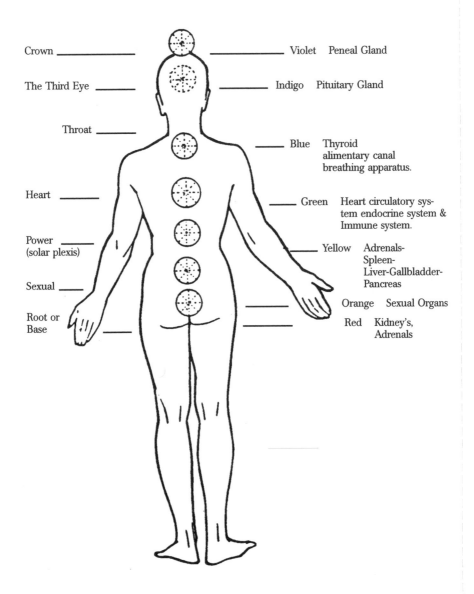

Crown _____ _____ Violet   Peneal Gland

The Third Eye _____ _____ Indigo   Pituitary Gland

Throat _____

Blue   Thyroid
alimentary canal
breathing apparatus.

Heart _____

Green   Heart circulatory system endocrine system &
Immune system.

Power _____
(solar plexis)

Yellow   Adrenals-
Spleen-
Liver-Gallbladder-
Pancreas

Sexual _____

Orange   Sexual Organs

Root or
Base

Red   Kidney's,
Adrenals

Adapted from Zachary F. Lansdowne, *The Chakras and Esoteric Healing* and Meredith Lady Young, *Agartha-A Journey to the Stars*.

Appendix C

Appendix C includes a detailed questionnaire for stress analysis entitled: Stress Questionnaire/Self-Analysis.

Stress Questionnaire

Self-Analysis

1. What is the first signal or cue from your body that you are feeling stressed?

   _____

2. How frequently do you feel stressed?
   ___ two to three times a day
   ___ two to three times a week
   ___ two to three times a month

3. What stress symptoms can you identify?

Physical
   ___ muscle knots, tightness or spasm
   ___ headaches
   ___ skin rashes
   ___ shortness of breath or difficulty breathing
   ___ dizziness, blurred vision
   ___ excessive tiredness
   ___ ulcers
   ___ colitis
   ___ chest pain
   ___ hypertension
   ___ other _____
   ___ _____
   ___ _____
   ___ _____
   ___ _____
   ___ _____
   ___ _____

Emotional

___ worry
___ nervousness
___ irritability
___ intense anger
___ general depression
___ fear
___ inappropriate humor
___ crying easily
___ other _____

_____
_____
_____
_____
_____
_____
_____

Behavioral

___ trouble making decisions
___ superficial involvement; appearance of giving
___ obvious time wasting
___ "unavailable" most of the time
___ overly precise
___ redrawing boundaries to shift or avoid responsibility
___ excessive drinking, smoking, or eating
___ absenteeism
___ other _____

_____
_____
_____
_____
_____
_____
_____

4. What specific situations are most likely to be stress producing for you? (Or where are you when you experience stress?)

_____

5. What specific individuals are difficult for you to deal with to the extent of producing stress? (List names.)

_____   _____

_____   _____

_____   _____

_____   _____

_____   _____

6. What kinds of requests are difficult to make?

_____

7. What kinds of refusals are difficult for you to express?

_____

8. Is it easy or difficult for you to
   a) give positive feedback   _____
   b) receive positive feedback   _____
   c) give negative feedback   _____
   d) receive negative feedback   _____

9. What stress do you believe you experience as a result of being a woman/man?

_____

10. Think of a time recently when you felt a significant amount of stress and describe it.
    What was the nature of the situation?
    Who were the people involved?
    What were your stress symptoms?
    What were the issues?
    What were the value questions?

What things occurred which may have contributed to
your stress?

Who are the individuals with whom you could openly
share these experiences?

_____

_____

_____

_____

_____

_____

_____

11. What do you currently do to cope with or manage
stress?

_____

_____

_____

12. Review your responses to the questionnaire. What patterns do you see emerging? Are you experiencing the
most stress at work or at home? Do you believe your
"stressors" are manageable or out of your control?

_____

_____

_____

Moore/Eddy 1980*

*The items in this questionnaire were derived from the
research and experience of Linda L. Moore and Bill Eddy.

BIBLIOGRAPHY

Austin, Nancy and Phelps, Stanlee. *The Assertive Woman.* Impact, SanLuis Obispo, 1975, 1987.

Belinkey, Mary Field; Clinchy, Blythe McVicker; Goldberger, Nancy Rule; Torule, Jill Mattuch. *Womens Ways of Knowing.* Basic Books, N.Y., 1986.

Cooper, Kenneth. *The Aerobics Program for Total Well-Being.* McGraw-Hill, New York, 1982.

Gendlin, Eugene. *Focusing.* New York, Bantam Books, 1981.

Gilligan, Carol. *In a Different Voice.* Harvard University Press, Cambridge, MA., 1982.

Goulding, Mary and Goulding, Robert. *Changing Lives Through Redecision Therapy.* Brunner/Mazel Publisher, New York, 1979.

Henning, Margaret and Jardim, Ann. *The Managerial Woman.* Doubleday, New York, 1981.

Josefowitz, Natasha. *Paths to Power.* Addison-Wesley, Reading MA., 1980.

Lansdowne, Zachary F. *The Chakras and Esoteric Healing.* Samuel Weiser, Inc. York Beach, Maine, 1986.

Lerner, Harriet Goldhor. *The Dance of Anger.* Harper and Row, New York, 1985.

Missildine, Hugh. *Your Inner Child of the Past.* New York, Pocket Books, 1963.

Patterson, Kerry; Grenny, Joseph; McMillan, Ron and Switzler, Al. *Crucial Conversations-Tools for Talking When Stakes Are High.*

Pollard, John K. *Self-Parenting.* Generic Human Studies Publishing, Malibu CA., 1987.

Ray, Sondra. *I Deserve Love.* Les Femmes, Millbrae, CA., 1976.

Schaef, Anne Wilson. *Womens Realities—An Emerging Female System in the White Male Society.* Winston Press, Inc., Minneapolis, 1981.

Sargent, Alice. *The Androgynous Manager.* AMACOM, a division of American Management Associations, New York, 1981.

Shaevitz, Marjorie. *The Superwoman Syndrome.* Warner Books, New York, 1984.

Subby, Robert and Friel, John. *Co-dependency and Family Rules.* Health Communications, Inc. Pompano Beach, Florida, 1984.

Warschau, Tesa Albert. *Winning by Negotiation.* Berkley Books, New York, 1981.

Welsh, Mary Scott. *Networking.* Harcourt, Brace, Jannovich, New York, 1980.

Whitfield, Charles. *Healing the Child Within.* Health Communications, Inc., Pompano Beach, Florida. 1987.